The Wills of Suffolk County Long Island [New York] Liber A 1787-1798

Abstracted by
George M. Easter

With a New Introduction by
Dr. Ellen Towne Skidmore

HERITAGE BOOKS
2007

HERITAGE BOOKS

AN IMPRINT OF HERITAGE BOOKS, INC.

Books, CDs, and more—Worldwide

For our listing of thousands of titles see our website
at
www.HeritageBooks.com

Published 2007 by
HERITAGE BOOKS, INC.
Publishing Division
65 East Main Street
Westminster, Maryland 21157-5026

International Standard Book Number: 978-0-7884-1703-7

CONTENTS

INTRODUCTION

The County of Suffolk was organized in 1683 and the Surrogate Court was formed there in 1787. Between those two dates wills were probated in New York City. Even after 1787 there were many who, in error, took their will out of the county for probate. These wills are to be found in the New York Historical Society Collections, which, if checked carefully for errata, are more to be trusted than Pelletreau's collection of Early Suffolk Wills taken from the Lester Wills, a MS in the County Clerk's Office at Riverhead.

Eardeley's Cemetery Inscriptions of Suffolk County contain a number of wills since 1737, and his Suffolk County wills is a selection of abstract and full copies collected through years of private research on certain families, also a list of wills recorded in the first few Libers. However, the present is the first serious attempt to make accessible in abstract form the wealth of genealogical information stored, most handsomely, in the modern county courthouse at Riverhead.

There are many things to remember when searching wills for those bright little facts which cast light on the past. I will mention those dealing with the witnesses. Their signatures may help in differentiating between them. I shall have to do something about that. It also helps to know who were the Clerks of the Surrogate Court, the physicians, schoolmasters, ministers and attorneys. For the period of this book, here are some of record. Surrogates: Thomas Tredwell, Jared Landon, Nicoll Floyd; physicians: Henry White, James Sandford, George Muirson Punderson, Ebenezer Sage, David Conkling, Daniel Robert, Silas Halsey, David Woodhull, Daniel Comstock, Samuel Thompson; minister: David Rose; attorney: Daniel Osborn; schoolmasters: John Stratton, John Curtis. These men often wrote the wills, witnessed their signing, swore to them and executed them. They were leading citizens. George Muirson may be a doctor.

George M. Easter

2

LIBER A.[1]

Liber A, Page 1. JOSEPH BURNET, 25 June 1787, gives land to son Joseph...other three boys 30 pounds when of age...girls to live in house until married...witnesses: Jonah Rogers. Jason Loper, Daniel Sherril. Proved 26 June 1787 by Jonas Rogers and Daniel Sherril of Southampton. Executrix appointed Arrezine Burnet, of Southampton, widow.

A-2. DANIEL WARNER, of Southold, 8 Oct. 1781, wife Hannah .... then to three sons, James, David and Benjamin, all under 21 years...daughters Deborah and Mehetabel Warner each 200 pounds...executrix, wife Hannah, with cousin James Reeve, executor ... witnesses: Daniel Wells, Matthew Beale, James Youngs. Proved 27 Mar.1787 by Daniel Wells and James Youngs of Southold. Administration granted 19 June 1787.

A-5. ABEL SWEZEY, of Brookhaven, 4 Sept.1779, "being very sick"...provides for wife Jerutia...gives lands in Brookhaven to sons Ezekiel and Mulford...Mulford to divide and Ezekiel to take his choice...to three other sons, Abel, Jeremiah and "my youngest son" 200 pounds apiece when 21 years...mentions mother Elizabeth...executors: Isaac Overton, Ezekiel Hedges and wife Jerutia ... witnesses: George Muirson, William Swezey, Henry Dayton...Proved 27 Mar. 1787 by William Swezey. Administration granted Isaac Overton 19 June 1797.

A-7. THOMAS OSBORN, of Easthampton, "taylor", 28 May 1787, "being indisposed"... provides for wife Phebe, son Abraham when 18, son Thomas when 14, and younger children's upbringing... to oldest son Abraham land bought of Elisha and

---

[1]All wills are originals unless prefixed cA-182 to denote a copy.

3

Eleazar Conkling, and of Burnet Miller, also land adjoining that of William and John Huntting...to son Jacob...to son Thoms land bought of Burnet Miller and Timothy Mulford, land adjoining that of Cornelius Osborn...to son Conkling... to son Lewis land adjoining that of Stephen Handspath...to daughter Phebe ten pounds...to daughter Jane 20 pounds...executors: Jeremiah Osborn and Abraham Barns ...witnesses John Chatfield, John Miller Jr., Thomas Jones. Proved 25June 1787 by John Chatfield and Thomas Jones "weaver" of Easthampton. Aministration granted 25 June 1787 to Jeremiah Osborn and Abraham Barns.

A-9. BARNABUS HORTON, of Southold. 29 Mar. 1787...provides for wife Susanne...mentions daughters and granddaughter Ann Wickham...to son Benjamin land...to son Gilbert land bought of Simon Moore...to son James 84 pounds...to son Jonathan 100 pounds...to granddaughters Rebecca, Susanna and Anna Horten five pounds when married...provides for daughter-in-law Rebecca Horton land, bought of John Overton...mentions grandsons Barnabus and Justus Horton, granddaughters Rebecca, Susan and Anna, and their father Barnabus Horton who purchased land of Nathan Moore at Goshen and sold to John Overton...executors sons Benjamin and Gilbert Horton ... witnesses: Elisha Dickerson, Samuel Dickerson, MehetabelBayley, John Hubbard. Proved 29 June 1787 by Elisha and Samuel Dickerson of Southold. Administration granted. 27 June 1787.

A-13. WILLIAM TURNER, of Brookhaven, "weak in body", 2 Jan. 1782 ...to son John five pounds...to son William lands, etc... provides for wife Catherine, his mother, son John and son William...executors: wife Catherine. Son William, and friend Reeve Howell ...witnesses: Henry Turner, Mary Sumrick, John Leeke. Proved 10 Aug. 1787 by John Leeke. Administration granted to Reeve Howell 10 Aug. 1787.

A-15. JACAMIAH ROGERS, of Huntington, 19 Apr. 1787, ... provides for wife, and children until of age...mentions daughters Rebecca, Ruth, Keturah and other daughters...to son Jacamiah ...children under age to be bound out at discretion of executors: Josiah Rogers. Thomas Ireland, Nathaniel Bunce... signed

4

JECAMIAH Rogers...witnesses: Thomas Rogers, Robert Rogers, James York. Proved 22 Aug.1787 by Thomas Rogers of Huntington. Administration granted 22 Aug.1787 to Thomas Ireland and Nathaniel Bunce.

A-17. GEORGE HAWKINS, of Brookhaven, 6 Feb. 1787, provides for wife Ruth Hawkins, son William, son Joseph, and daughter Mary while single...executors: wife Ruth, son William Hawkins, and Joseph S. Hawkins...signed 10 Feb. 1783...witnesses: Jonas Davis, Philip Smith, John Bennett. Proved 27 Nov. 1787 by Jonas Davis of Brookhaven. Administration granted 27 Nov. 1787 to William and Joseph S. Hawkins.

A-19. JOHN ROE, of Brookhaven, 7 Sept.1787...mentions land adjoining that of Philip Roe...gives two sons and two daughters, John, Asel, Anne and Mary Roe, estate equally divided... executors: wife Ruth Roe, brother Justus Roe, and cousin Phillip Roe...witnesses: Nathaniel Davis, James Davis, Nathaniel Tooker Jr. Proved 4 Dec. 1787 by James Davis of Brookhaven. Administration granted 4 Dec. 1787 to Justus Roe and Philip Roe.

A-20. NATHANIEL SMITH, of Islip, 27 Job. 1787...provides for wife "till she shall arive [sic] at age,...also two sons Philip and Walter Smith "till they arive [sic] at age...also three daughters, Sarah, Rachel and Charlotte Smith...executors: brother Philip Smith, brother-in-law Joseph Bunce, and Hennery Ludle, and cousin Thome Udal...witnesses: Jacob Willets, Jedidiah Williamson, John Willets. Proved 5 Dec. 1787 by Jacob Willets of Islip "a quaker." Administration granted 5 Dec. 1787 to Henry Ludlam.

A-22. JOHN MORGAN, of Huntington, 31 July 1787, "in dangerous state of health" provides for wife and for bringing up children...paper mill to be sold... friends Jonas Rogers. Eliphelet Jervis, and wife Elisabeth Morgan...witnesses: Daniel Wiggins, William Lysaght. Proved 10 Dec. 1787 by William Lysaght of Huntington,shipwright. Administration granted 10 Dec. 1787 to Eliphelet Jervis and Elizabeth Morgan.

A-24. JEMIMAH LANE, widow, of Southampton, 14 Oct. 1787...gives grandson William Lane Williamson lands and etc...remembers granddaughter Elisabeth Williamson...Executors: nephew Samuel Jennings and daughter Jemima Williamson...witnesses: David Haines Foster, Henry White. Proved 25 Dec. 1787 by David Haines Foster and Henry White "physician" of Southampton. Administration granted to Samuel Jennings 25 Dec. 1787.

A-25. SILAS HOWELL, of Southampton, 2 Juno 1787...gives lot promised by grandfather to cousin Matthew Howell Jr...gives cousin David Howell windmill and land at Shinicock Neck...gives to cousin Silas Howell, son of Stephen Howell, home and etc...gives brother David Howell land bought of George Herrick, and of Jerebel Howell...gives cousin Silas Howell,son of Stephen Howell, land bought of Ezekiel Howell Jr...gives cousin Stephen Howell rights in Sag Harbor and land where Capt. Joseph Ellis' house stood...to Malby Geilston 40 pounds...to Abigail Herrick 15 pounds...to cousin Silas Howell in Gearses [Jersey?] 300 pounds... to cousin Abraham 100 pounds...to brother Charles Howells children 20 pounds each...cousin David Howell 100 pounds...cousin Stephen Howell 300 pounds...executors: Hugh Geilston and Stephen Howell... witnesses: Silvanus Howell. William Halloick, Ebenezer Jessup...Proved 24 Dec. 1787 by Silvanus Howell "shipjoiner" and William Halloick "farmer," both of Southhampton. Administration granted 27 Dec, 1787 to Hugh Gelston and Stephen Howell.

A-27. EBENEZER HAVENS, of Shelter Island, 5 May 1787...executors to sell moveables...gives niece Deborah Parker, daughter of sister Hannah Parker, deceased 20 pounds...gives reminder to nephew Augustus Havens, son of brother Jos. Havens... executors: brother Joseph Havens, friends William Bowditch and James Havens... witnesses: Ephraim King, Benjamin Conkling, Clarinda Buchannan. Proved 27 Dec.1787 by Ephraim King. Administration granted 27 Dec. 1787 to Joseph Havens and William Bowditch.

A-29. EBENEZER WHITE, of Southampton, farmer, 24 Jan. 1783...very sick...provides for wife Mehetable White...orders son

6

James White in her behalf...to daughter Hannah Howell 30 pounds... to daughter Mehetable Hildreth 30 pounds... to daughter Jerusha Havens 30 pounds... two grandsons Silas and James White to get five pounds each...all else to son James White...executors; wife Mehetable and son James White...witnesses: Lemuel Halsey, Jasper Jennings, Joseph Gibbs. Proved 27 Dec. 1787 by Lemuel Halsev of Southampton. Administration granted 27 Doe.1797 to James White.

A-32. SUSANNAH COOPER, relict of Thomas Cooper, of Southampton, 16 Oct. 1796...very sick...gives to daughter Clarissa and son Thomas...executors: brothers John Cooper, Isaac Post and Caleb Cooper...witnesses: Caleb Cooper, Isaac Post, Elisabeth Cooper. Proved 25 Dec. 179 by Caleb Cooper and Elisabeth Cooper "spinster" both of Southampton, Administration granted 28 Dec.1797 to John and Caleb Cooper.

A-34. JONATHAN BRUSH, of Huntington, 22 Sept-1786...executors to sell all land and etc...provides for wife Elisabeth...gives daughter Hebzibah "all linen she has made since other daughters left home"...four sons now living...sons Smith, Daniel, Josiut and Robert Brush and daughter Hepzibah Brush 20 pounds each...mentions children of son Joshua deceased... executors: three sons Smith, Daniel and Robert Brush...witnesses: John Buffet, Elisabeth Potter, Jacamiah Brush. Proved I Jan. 17SS by John Buffet of Huntington. Administration granted I Jan.1788 to Smith Brush, Daniel Brush and Robert Brush.

A-36. PHILIP SCIDMORE, of Huntington, 24 Mar. 1785...gives to wife Margaret all moveables, lands to be sold, interest thereof to go for support of two sons until aged 21... eldest son Joel when 21 to have portion of principle...younger son Platt when 21 to have his share...executors: wife Margaret, friends Melancton Bryant and Henry Scudder...witnesses: Epenetus Smith, Jonas Gildersleeve, David Wood. Proved 5 Apr. 1786 by Epenetus Smith. Henry Scudder wrote the will. Administration granted 1 Jan. 1788 to Margaret Scidmore.

A-39. JAMES BISHOP, of Huntington, 20 Dec. 1787...gives wife

Susanna and daughter Jemimah household furniture etc...gives daughter Abigail one pound, and her second son Samuel four pounds ... gives son John dwelling and land had of Isaac Smith...remembers son Jonah and son Hennery...gives daughter Jemima 30 pounds... executors: Jesse Bryan and Thomas White Gildersleeve...witnesses: Epenetus Wood, Epenetus Smith, William Jarvis...Proved 3 Jan. 1788 by Epenetus Wood of Smithtown,"weaver", and Epenetus Smith of Huntington. Administration granted 3 Jan 1788 to Jesse Bryan and Thomas Whited Gildersleeve.

A-41. DAVID CONKLING, of Southold, 27 May 1787, ... mentions father John Conkling deceased...gives David Conkling, son of brother Jacob Conkling, bulk of property when 21...mentions other sons of brother Jacob Conkling... to brother Stephen Conkling...to Gamaliel, son of brother Jacob. eight pounds when 21. ..to four sisters ... executors: Stephen Conkling and brother-in-law Jared Landon... witnesses: Elijah Landon, Mary Landon, Bethiah Landon. Proved 7 Jan.1788 by Elijah and Mary Landon and Bethiah Landon "spinster", of Southold. Administration granted 7 Jan. 1788 to Jared Landon.

A-43. RICHARD CONKLING, of Huntington, 23 July 1787,..executors to sell land formerly of John Titus and the parsonage...provides for wife...gives two daughters Rebecca and Jemima 20 pounds each... gives daughter Elizabeth 30 pounds.. .remembers five sons Titus, Richard, Henry, Enoch and Beuel Conkling...executors: brother-in-law Capt. Jonathan Titus and sons Titus and Richard Conkling...witnesses: James Sandford, Rosana Keen, Jacob Titus. Proved 5 Apr. 1788 by James Sandford "physician" of Huntington. Aministration granted 5 Apr, 1788 to Jonathan Titus and Richard Conkling.

A-45. JOSEPH WHITE, of Huntington, 22 Oct. 1781...estate to wife Sarah White until she marries again or dies, then to the children of brothers and sisters Phebe Whitman, Charity Jarvis, Stevan White and Sarah Colyer...executors: friend Amos Whitson and Sealah Wood of Huntington, and wife Sarah White...witnesses: John Whitson, Daniel Pearsall, Jarvis Whitman. Proved 17 Apr. 1788 by John Whitson, quaker.

Administration granted 17 Apr. 1788 to Amos Whitson and Selah Wood.

A-48. ELEAZER MILLER, of Easthampton, 26 Apr. 1786...gives son Burnet Miller five shillings...other legacies to son Jeremiah Miller, son Eleazer Miller, son Ananias Miller; three daughters Mary Hedges, Jemima Talmage, Mehitabel Baker; two grandsons Thomas Jones and Eleazer Jones, and son Abraham Miller...executors: son Abraham Miller and sons-in-law Thomas Talmage and Stephen Hedges ... witnessesd: Thomas Wickham, Nathan Conkling Jr.,John Stratton. Proved 25 Apr. 1788 by Thomas Wickham and John Stratton of Easthampton. Administration granted 25 Lpr.1788 to Abraham Miller and Stephen Hedges.

A-50. JOB PIERSON,of Southampton, 10 Aug. 1779...gives son Lemuel Pierson lana bought of Peter Hildreth and David Hand, also land adjoining that of James Hains...mentions land sold to John Rusel...gives son David Pierson land adjoining that of David Hedges, and John Pierson, deceased...mentions Negro Petter...gives daughters 200 pounds each...gives grandson Samuel Pierson 50 pounds...grand-daughter Margaret Satherly to have 100 pounds...gives granddaughter CatherinePierson 50 pounds...gives granddaughter Hannah Baron a tankard...remembers granddaughter Mary Baron...executors: two sons Lemuel and David Pierson and friend David Topping...witnesses: John Davis, Abraham Howall, Daniel Pierson. Proved 26 Apr. 1788 by John Davis "cordwainer" and Abraham Howell both of Southampton. Administration granted 26 Apr. 1788 to Lemuel and David Pierson.

A-52. THEOPHILUS HALSEY, of Southampton, 18 Mar. 1788... provides for wife...gives all to children Phebe, Mary and Asintha Halsey...executors: wife Phebe Halsey and Walter Howell...witnesses: Joshua Hildreth, Josiah Cooper, William Halsey. Proved 26 Apr. 1788 by Joshua Hildreth and Josiah Cooper, cordwainers, of Southampton. Administration granted 26 Apr. 1788 to Walter Howell.

9

A-53. MARTHA SANDFORD, of Southampton, at that place 27 Dec. 1787...gives to three children, son James Mungomery, son John Monmoth, daughter Sarah Sandford, with 10 pounds to daughter Sarah, all the estate...mentions husband's will of 20 Dec. 1785... executors: Samuel Haines, Samuel Howell of Mecox, also to be guardians of children...witnesses: Proculah Cook, Stephen S. Topping, John Cook. Proved 26 ADr. 1788 by John Cook and Proculah Cook, spinster, both of Southampton. Administration granted 26 Apr. 1788 to Samuel Haines and Samuel Howell.

A-55. JOHN CARMAN, of Half Hollow Hills, Huntington, 21 Jan. 1782..."advanced in years"...gives daughter Elizabeth Carman 140 pounds in trust to executors ... to four daughters Margaret Chichester, Sarah Brush, Phebe Nostran and Mary Rolph the remainder of personal property...gives two sons John and Samuel Carman lands equally divided... executors: sons John and Samuel Carman and son-in-law Jacobus Nostran...witnesses: John Ruland, David Ruland, Wilmot Oakley. Proved 20 lav 1788 by Wilmot Oakley of Huntington. Administration granted 20 May 1788 to John and Samuel Carman and Jacobus Nostran.

A-57. MOSES VAIL, of Huntington, 22 Mar. 1785...mentions two sons John and Micah Vail...wife Deborah provided for...remembers daughter Phebe Canef and daughter Elizabeth Brush...son Micah to have the hog ponds which Simon Fleet claims...executors: John and Micah Vail...witnesses: John Stratton, John Scudder, John Fleet. Proved 24 May 1788 by John Stratton of Smithtown and John Scudder of Huntington. Administration granted 24 May 1788 to John and Micah Vail.

A-59. TIMOTHY SCUDDER, of Crabmeadow in Huntington, 7 Nov. 1778...gives son Timothy Scudder land adjoining that of Augustine Bryan, of Melancthon Bryan, of widow Bryan, of Austin Jarvis, of Simon Fleet...gives son Henry Scudder land at Cow Harbor formerly of brother John Scudder, deceased...gives grandson Tredwell Scudder lands at Musketucks...Tredwell and brothers of his, John and Jesse under age ... they have two sisters Hannah and Sarah Scudder, all children of daughter-in-law Sarah Scudder, widow of son Joel...executors to be guardians of John and Jesse, grandsons, and to put them to trades...gives Timothy and Ananias Carll 20 pounds...remembers four daughters Jemima Rusco, Hannah Carll, Jerusha Carll and Sarah Buffet...executors: son Henry Scudder and sons-in-law Timothy and Ananias Carll. ..witnesses: Philip Ketcham, Conkling Ketcham, Solomon Ketcham. Proved 20 May 1788 by Conkling Ketcham and Philip Ketcham separately. Administration granted 20 May 1788 to Henry Scudder and Timothy and Ananias Carill.

A-63. DAVID FITHIN HALSEY, of Southampton, 24 June 1788...gives daughter Clarissa 25 pounds...estate to son Henry Halsey...gives other two daughters Lucindia and Polly 25 pounds...executors: friends Silvenus Halsey, son of Timothy Halsey, and Jonathan Rogers both of Southampton...witnesses: David Haines Foster,Oliver Clark, Stephen Gooale. Proved 27 Aug. 1788 by David Raines Poster and Oliver Clark "sailor" both of Southampton. Administration granted to both Silvenus Halsey and Jonathan Rogers 27 Aug. 1788.

A-64. JAMES BROWN, of Southampton, 4 Apr. 1787...gives to wife whole estate...to three daughters Elizabeth, Sarah and Mary five shillings each...gives son Samuel five shillings...executrix: "my wife"...witnesses: Aaron Woolworth, David Sayre, John Gelston. Proved 27 Aug. 1789 bv David Sayre "joiner" and John Gelston both of Southampton. Administration granted 28 Aug. 1788 to Mrs. Brown.

A-66. SILAS FOSTER, of Southhold, 27 Sept. 1775...gives everything, to sister Hannah Foster...executors: friends Ephraim Howell and David Haines Foster...witnesses: George Mackie, John Goldsmith, Joseph Goldsmith. Proved 28 Aug.1788 by Joseph Goldmith, blacksmith of Southampton. Administration granted, 28 Aug. 1788 to Ephraim Howell and David Haines Foster.

A-67. BENJMIN CASE, of Southold, 6 June 1775...estate first to wife Esther Case and then to children Benjamin, Ichabod, Daniel and Gilbert Case "as tenants in common and not in jointenancy"... remembers daughters...executors: two sons Benjamin and Gershom Case... witnesses: Daniel Osborn Jr., Benjamin Moore, and Benjamin Paine. Proved 30 Aug. 1788 by Daniel Osborne Jr. of Southold. Administration granted 30 Aug. 1788 to Gershom Case.

A-69. WILLIAM HORTON, of Southold, 5 May 1782...to son William Horton...provides for present wife Mary...gives son Jonathan Horton lend at Indian Neck bought of Joshua Horton...remembers daughters Mary Vail, Hannah Vail, Bethiah Weells and "the two daughters of my daughter Phebe, deceased...to niece Mehetable Horton the gifts from "my.brother Moses Horton, deceased"...remembers Patience, wife of son William Horton...executors: two sons William and Jonathan Horton ... witnesses: Micah Horton, Elten Overton, James Whelock Booth. Proved 9 Oct. 1788 by James Whelock Booth of Southold. Administration granted William and Jonathan Horton 9 Oct.1788.

A-71. EZEKIEL HOWELL, of Southampton, 12 Aug. 1778...to mother Deborah Howell estate for life, then to three sisters Eunice, Anna and Prudence Horton...executors: Eunice, Anna and Prudence Horton...witnesses: Joshua Hildreth, Margaret Pierson, Joseph Gibbs. Proved 10 Oct. 1788 by Joshua Hildreth,cordwainer,of Southampton. Administration granted 10 Oct. 1788 to Eunice and Prudence Horton.

A-73. RICHARD WOODHULL, of Brookhaven, 7 June1788...provides for wife Margaret Woodhull...gives grandson Richard Woodhull land where Thomas Mount lately lived, adjoining confiscated land of late Dowr. George Muiason, also land of Widow Bennet, of Daniel Satterly...gives granddaughter Dorothy Woodhull 34 pounds when 18 ...gives granddaughter Julia Woodhull 33 pounds when 18...gives granddaughter Sarah Woodhull 33 pounds when 18...gives daughter Susanna Woodhull five shillings...gives daughter Mary Underhill 200 pounds...remembers son Abraham...executors: wife Margaret Woodhull, son Abraham Woodhull and Judge Selah Strong ... witnesses; Jonathan Dickerson, Daniel Satterly, John Curtis. Proved 28 Oct.1788 by Daniel Satterly of

Brookhaven. Administration granted 28 Oct. 1788 to Abraham Woodhull and Selah Strong.

A-76. JOSEPH POWELL, of Huntington, verbally 12 Feb. 1789 at house of Jesse Brundage after being mortally injured by falling timber while taking down frame house...reminds heirs to give Jesse Brundage the deed to his land...lands and etc. to be divided between two sons, moveables between daughters. Recorded 16 Feb. 1789 by Samuel Powell [Ed. probable son?], John Merrit, Joshua Corvell, Scudder Robbins, Amos Powell [Ed. probable son?]. Proved 19 Mar.1789 by Samuel Powell and John Merrit of Oyster Bay and Scudder Robbins of Huntington "weaver." Administration granted 19 Mar.1789 to Jacob Covert of Huntington, husband of Catharine a daughter and legatee of Joseph Powell.

A-78. THOMAS UDALL, of Huntington South. 21 Jan. 1788...provides for wife Sukey Udall "untill my youngest son Charles arrives to the age of twenty one"... gives daughter Sarah Udall 50 pounds when married or of age of 21, and 150 pounds when 23...reminder of estate to two sons Richard and Charles Udall.. .executors: wife and friends Charles Valentine, David Valentine and Richard Udall Sr...witnesses: Jacob Valentine Jr., Jacob Colwell, Lewis Valentine. Proved 17 Mar. 1789 by Jacob Valentine Jr. of Huntington. Administration granted 21 Mar. 1789 to Richard Udall Sr.

A-80. SAMUEL LEWIS, of Long Swamp in Huntington, 8 Mar. 1788...provides for wife Nansa Lewis and for children's bringing up until youngest to 14...gives daughter Asenth (Aseneth) her mother's, his first wife's, things and also ten pounds...proceeds from sale of land at Southside and Wolf Hill to go equally to five sons Eleanah, Thomas Bunce, Daniel, John, Joseph Lewis...executors to be guardians of children and to bind out sons to trades...executors: friends Philip Smith, Zadock Smith, Josiah Smith...witnesses; Jesse Kellam, Joshua Kellam, Eliphelet Bunce, Ananias Carll. Proved 23 Mar. 1789 by Ananias Carll "blacksmith" of Huntington. Administration granted 23 Mar.1789 to Philip, Zadock and Josiah Smith.

A-82. JAMES OVERTON, of Brookhaven, 20 Apr. 1785...estate to son Benjamin, provided he gives each sister five pounds when of age...provides for wife Phebe Overton, who signs with him... executors: Nathaniel and Messenger Overton, brothers of Brookhaven..witnesses: Justus Overton. Deborah Overton. Prove22 Nov. 1788 by Justus Overton. Nathanial and Messenger Overton relinquish executorship... Administration granted 24 Mar. 1789 to the widow, Phebe Overton.

A-85. THOMAS SANDFORD, of Southampton, 7 Dec. 1785...provides for wife Phobe Sandford and her family...mentions land bought of Joshua Rogers, also property wife had when married...gives son Thomas Sandford 1200 pounds...gives son Nathan Sandford land in Easthampton...gives three granddaughters Phebe, Susanah and Mary Miller 300 pounds each, and furniture that was their grandmother Sandford's...gives daughter Phebe Sandford 500 pounds...gives three children Thomas, Nathan and Phebe Sandford money left over... executors: wife Phebe Sandford and friend David Hains... witnesses: Joseph Goldsmith, Daniel Sandford, Jesse Hallsey. Proved 27 Mar. 1789 by Joseph Goldsmith "blacksmith" and Daniel Sandford "carpenter" and Jesse Hallsey, all of Southampton. Administration granted 27 Mar. 1789 to Mrs. Phebe Sandford and David Hains.

A-87. NATHAN CONKLING JR., of Easthampton, 11 Feb. 1788... provides for daughter Elizabeth and for cousin Mary Osborn while single...gives reminder to only son Jonathan...executors: cousin Jacob Hedges, friend Ludlam Parsons, cousin Mary Osborn... witnesses: Jesse Dayton, William Mulford, John Stratton. Proved 28 Mar. 1789 by Jesse Dayton "hatter" and John Stratton, both of Easthampton. Ad-ministration granted 28 Mar. 1789 to Jacob Hedges and Ludlam Parsons.

A-89. JEMIMA WICK, of Southampton, 10 Oct. 1788. . .gives estate to son John ...gives daughter 12 pounds when 21...mentions "my two children when of age...gives daughter Jemima apparel of her sisters that died...wishes daughter to live with her aunt Abigail Jager till of age...executor: John Fordham...witnesses: Lucretia Mason, Josiah Colburn. Nathan

14

Fordham. Proved 30 Mar. 1789 by Nathan Fordham. Administration granted 30 Mar. 1789 to John Fordham.

A-90. JOSHUA CLARK, of Southold, 21 Feb. 1789...provides for wife Molly Clark ... gives nephew Henry Hudson 200 pounds...gives Hannah Beale 50 pounds...gives nephew Samuel L. Clark 50 pounds...gives Samuel Clark, son of Samuel L.Clark, 50 pounds...gives negro man Lymas his freedom, 100 pounds and all coopors, joiners, blacksmith and carpenters tools...orders Henry Hudson, Samuel L. Clark and Samuel Clark to give bonds preventing Lymas becoming chargeable to the town...gives remainder of property equally divided to Nathan Benjamin, Benjamin Clark, Mary Cleavs, Martha Conkling, Sarah Bushop and Puah Smith... executors: Benjamin Goldsmith, Capt. Joshua Benjamin and "my wife Molly Clark...witnesses: Richard S. Hubbard Jr., John Hart, David Harvey. Proved 6 Apr. 1789by Richard S. Hubbard Jr.,John Hart, David Harvey, all coopers of Southold. Administration granted 6 Apr. 1789 to Benjamin Goldsmith, Joshua Benjamin, and Molly Clark.

A-92. SARAH HUDSON, of Southold, 27 Jan. 1789.. gives cousin Richard Brown lands and etc...remembers Richard Brown's daughter Deborah...remembers Desire, wife of Richard Brown...executors: Reubin Brown, cousin Richard Brown ...witnesses: Francois Fournier, Deborah Fournier, Matthew Beale. Proved 7 Apr. 1789 by Deborah Fournier "spinster" of Southold. Administration granted 7 Apr. 1789 to Richard Brown.

A-94. ISAACSMITH, of Brookhaven, 12 May 1787...provides for wife Martha...two sons Joshua and Isaac Smith charged with her care... gives Joshua Smith land at Coram...gives grandaughter Margaret Smith, daughter of son Joshua Smith, and Fanny, daughter of Joshua Smith, lands at Chestnut Pond, Corum...mentions son Joshua Smith and his wife...gives grandsons Every, John and Japhat, sons of son Isaac Smith, homestead and land adjoining that of Caleb Mapes Hulse, David Overton and Joseph Ruland...mentions son Isaac Smith and his wife...executors: Caleb Mapes Hulse, Nathaniel Overton...witnesses: Palmer Overton, Isaac Hulse, John Overton. Proved 8 Apr. 1799 by Palmer and John Overton. Administration granted 8 Apr. 1789 to Caleb Mapes Hules and Nathaniel Overton.

A-97. NATHANIEL ROE, of Brookhaven, 11 Jan. 1760...reserves to wife her dowry... gives son Phillups land...gives son Nathaniel homestead land adjoining that of Col. Floyd, Justice Strong, Mr. Jones, John Roe, Mr. Miller and Mr. Tooker, also land bought of Jacob Longbottom...gives two sons Phillips and Nathaniel remaining lands between them...gives two younger sons James and William 100 pounds each when of age and to be put to trades at 16...gives four daughters Sarah, Hannah, Elisabeth and Deborah 25 pounds and an additional 10 pounds in 1770 each...pay debt owing daughter Hannah... provides for daughter Sarah when married same as already done for Hannah, Elisabeth and Deborah...Sarah, while single, to have room "my mother died in"...executors: brother John Roe and Phillups and Nathaniel Roe...witnesses: John Roe, Benjamin Tallmdge, Zipporah Tallmadge. ..codicil 6 Feb. 1774... witnesses: Benjamin Tallmadge, Zipporah Tallmadge, John Tallmadge. Proved so Apr. 1789 by Nathaniel Davis "shopkeeper" and Charity Roe. widow, when nine persons appeared and Benjamin Tallmadge's signature was sworn to be authentic by Nathaniel Davis and Phillips Roe,Jr., and in testimony of Phillips Roe the only surviving executor. Administration granted 30 Apr. 1789 to Phillips Roe.

A-102. NATHANIEL ROE JR., of Brookhaven, 12 Nov. 1782...gives wife 100 pounds and negro wench and negro boy...gives son a double portion...mentions other children...executors; wife and Nathaniel Davis and Ebenezer Miller...witnesses: James Roe, Phillips Roe Jr. Proved 30 Apr. 1789 by Phillips Roe Jr. Administration granted 30 Apr. 1789 to Nathaniel Davis and Ebenezer Miller.

A-103. WILLIAM CLARK, of Brookhaven, 17 Sept. 1792...provides for wife for life... gives grandson William Clark, now under age, the inheritance...mentions son, William, the child's father deceased... remembers grandson Jonathan Tarry and "my daughters" Mary, Hannah, Bathsheba, Deliverance and Puah...provides for daughter-in-law Phebe Clark for bringing up of the heir and his

16

sisters...remembers daughters Mary, Hannah, Bathsheba, Deliverance and Puah, and the oldest female heir of daughter Deborah deceased, and granddaughter Hannah Clark...executors: daughter Phebe Clark, friend John Leek... witnesses: Isaac Robbins, Jean Jones, John Leek. Proved 24 Mar. 1789 by Isaac Robbins " carpenter" and John Leek "blacksmith" both of Brookhaven. Administration granted 24 Mar. 1789 to Phebe Clark and John Leek.

A-l05. RACHEL D'HONNEUR, formerly of Suffolk County now residing in New York City, Aug. 1782...estate to be sold... a third goes to granddaughter Gloriana Margaretta, wife of John Loudon McAdam...a third goes to granddaughter Joanna Rachael Nicoll...a third goes to William Rhinelander and John Loudon McAdam "auctioneers" and Andrew Underhill "merchant" of Now York City in trust for the use for life of granddaughter Charity Kettletas, wife of Garret Kettletas, and at her death to be divided between her children... gives negro servant Moll her freedom... executors: William Rhinelander, John Loudon McAdam and Andrew Underhill...witnesses: Grove Bend, Heathcote Johnston, Ward Chipman. Proved 25 Apr. 1789 by Grove Bend "merchant" of New York City. Administration granted 25 Apr. 1789 to William Rhinelander.

A-107. ZEBULON ROBBINS, of Brookhaven, 3 Oct. l788...provides for wife Suannah Robbins...gives Caroline Church, Brookhaven, 100 pounds...gives Robert Jayne Sr. of Brookhaven 100 pounds...gives brother Isaac Robbins' eldest son remainder of estate...executors: friends Robert Jayne Sr., Isaac Robbins and Susannah Robbins... witnesses: Charles Dallas, Richard Dewick, George M. Punderson. Proved I May 1789 by George Muirson Puderson "physician" (who swore to writing will under instructions by Zebulon Robbins, and that he mistakenly called Isaac a brother of testator thinking it was so) and by Charles Dallas and Richard Dewick (who, not remembering hearing the signing or sealing of will yet that Zebulon was so weak and when asked he assented to the will). Administration granted 6 May 1789 to Isaac Robbins. (For earlier will see A-107* at end of Liber A.)

A-110. ABRAHAM SMITH, of Brookhaven, verbally 4 Feb. 1789...gives wife Elizabeth half estate, and daughter Jane other half...executrix: wife Elizabeth... witnesses: who recorded it 18 May 1789 William Smith, Barnabas Smith, Seth Scribner. Proved 18 May 1789 by William Smith, Barnabas Smith "farmer" and Seth Scribner "cordwainer" all of Brookhaven. Administration granted 18 May 1789 to Elizabeth Smith.

A-112. JESSE ROGERS, of Islip, 25 Jan. 1780...provides for wife Marcy Rogers a place called Nipscop and half the land at Great Neck and Huntington South...gives daughter Jemima Rogers until of age other half of land to be hired out...gives sons Jesse Rogers and Jonathan Rogers lands in Huntington and Islip...executors: brother John Rogers, friends John Oakley and John Pratt...signed by wife also...witnesses: Platt Wheler, Selah Dingee, Sarah Wheler. Proved 3 June 1789 by Platt Wheeler of Smithtown and Selah Dingee of Huntington. Administration granted 3 June 1789 to John Oakley and John Rogers.

A-114. EPENETUS BRYAN, of Huntington, 27 Mar. 1784...provides for wife Rhoda...gives son Azel 200 pounds...two sons Lemuel and Jesse directed to pay it when he is 21, and to care for him and put him to a trade...executors to sell land formerly of brother Alexander Bryan, proceeds to divide between son Azel and two daughters Jemima Cells and Mary Grice... remainder to divide between three grandchildren Nathaniel, John and Stratton Bryan...executors: two sons Lemuel and Jesse Bryan, and Melancthon Bryan...witnesses: Henry Scudder, Carll Ketcham, Silas Newman. Proved 25 June 1789 by Henry Scudder and Carll Ketcham. Administration granted 25 June 1789 to Lemuel and Jesse Bryan.

A-117. NATHANIEL TOOKER, of Brooklhamiton, I Aug. 1783...gives estate Equally divided to Nathaniel and Thomas Tooker "my two sons"...executors: Timothy Norton, wife Ruth Tooker and Selah Strong...witnesses: William Shelton, Shadrack Kelley, Thomas Strong...Proved 27 June 1787 by Thomas Strong. Administration granted 27June 1787 to Selah Strong.

18

A-119. NEHEMIAH SAYER, of Southampton, 20 July 1784...provides wife Bethiah with dower...gives three daughters Elizabeth, Hannah and Jane 29 pounds each...gives son John Sayre bed and five pounds...gives son James Sayre 200 pounds and half the land at Susquehanah...gives son Abraham Sayre land at Southampton, charged with support of son John...mentions will of children's grandfather...executor: son Abraham Sayre...witnesses: George Mackie, David Burnet, Isaac Post. Proved I July 1789 by George Mackie "cooper". Administration granted I July 1789 to Abraham Sayre.

A-121. HENRY HARRIS, of Southampton, 28 Aug. 1787...Provides for wife Abigail Harris...gives eldest son David Harris half of lands etc .... gives second son Henry Harris half of lands etc...gives third son Elias Harris 50 pounds and two sons David and Henry are to put him to a trade...gives oldest daughter Anna Howell ten pounds...gives daughter Mary Jennings and daughter Jane Harris 40 shillings each...gives daughter (fourth) Sarah Harris clothing of her own mother and 40 shillings...executors: sons David and Henry Harris... witnesses: David Haines Foster, Daniel Harris, David Rose. Proved I July 1789 by David Haines Foster and David Rose. Administration granted I July 1789 to David and Henry Harris.

A-123. JESSE CULVER, of Southampton. 9 July 1782...provides for wife Phebe...gives son Moses Culver land adjoining that of Jeremiah Culver, and John Halsey....gives son Zephaniah Culver 40 shillings... gives son Edward Culver five pounds... gives two daughters Mary Reeves and Hannah Mackie five shillings each...gives daughter Mehetable Culver five pounds and home with mother until married... executors: son Moses Culver and friend Caleb Cooper...witnesses: Obadiah Cooper, Ephraim l'Hommedieu, Stephen Rogers. Proved I July 1789 by Obadiah Cooper "carpenter". Administration granted I July 1789 to Moses Culver and Caleb Cooper.

A-126. JOHN NORRIS, of Southampton, 25 Jan. 1786...provides for wife Sarah Norris...gives son John Norris lands etc...gives daughter Alice Norris five shillings and a home until married...gives daughters Kesiah Flint, Sarah Edwards, Hannah

Hatch and Phebe Hillock five shillings each...executor: son John Norris...witnesses: Daniel Howell, Price Howell, Simon Howell. Proved 8 Oct. 1789 by Daniel Howell and Price Howell "cooper". Administration granted 8 Oct. 1789 to son John Norris.

A-127. SAMUEL HOWELL, of Southampton, 14 Sept. 1782...provides for wife Sarah ... gives son Lemuel Howell lands at Canoeplace, Kitchabonuck, Red Creek...gives four daughters Hannah Fordham, Prudence Hulbert, Eunice Babbit and Marah Foster five pounds each...gives daughter Mebetabal Howell 40 pounds...gives grandson James Fordham ten pounds...gives Ephraim Howell dwelling house...reminder of moveables to wife Sarah and daughter Sarah Howell, the latter to live in house until married...executors: two sons Ephraim and Lemuel Howell... witnesses: David Howell, Silas Poster, Henry Herrick. Proved 8 Oct. 1789 by David Howell.Administration granted 8 Oct. 1789 to Ephraim and Lemuel Howell.

A-130. ABRAHAM MULFORD, of Easthampton, 30 Dec. 1786...wife is provided for...gives daughter Phebe 20 pounds and maintenance... gives three eldest daughters Mary, Rebekah and Abigail 20 shillings each...gives son Abraham Mulford half estate...land in Ackaboneck, Montauk...mentions land from father now owned by brother Lemuel...gives son Samuel half estate...executors: two sons Abraham and Samuel Mulford...witnesses: Nathaniel Dominy, Nathaniel Dominy Jr., John Stratton. Proved 9 Oct. 1789 bv Nathaniel Dominy "clockmaker", Nathaniel Dominy "carpenter". Administration granted 9 Oct. 1789 to Abraham and Samuel Mulford.

A-132. SAMUEL JAYNE, of Brookhaven, I Oct. 1789...gives daughter Elizabeth Jayne 20 pounds...gives on Samuel Jayne all else... executors: wife Elizabeth Jayne and son Samuel Jayne... signed by Samuel JANE...witnesses: Ame Bennet, William Jayne Jr., John Curtis. Proved 9 Nov. 1,789 by William Jayne Jr. Administration granted 9 Nov. 1789 to Samuel Jayne.

A-134. EBENEZER MILLER, of Brookhaven, 16 Apr. 1789...gives wife Sarah Miller use of estate while son Isaac is single... gives son Isaac lands ..gives daughter Martha Miller 30 pounds...gives daughter Clarisia Miller 80 pounds when of age, with house room while single...gives son Benajah S. Miller 80 pounds when of age... executors: wife Sarah, Capt. Merit S. Woodhull., and son-in-law Nathaniel Miller...witnesses: Caleb Woodhull, Nathaniel Davis, Zophar M. Millar. Proved 22 Dec. 1789 by Caleb Woodhull and Nathaniel Davis "merchant". Administration granted 22 Dec. 1789 to Merrit Smith Woodhull and Nathaniel Miller.

A-137. JAMES REEVE of Southold, 11 Nov. 1788...gives wife Anna full dower...to support four children, excepting James and John...gives third son John Reeve land adjoining that of brother Isaac and Barnabus Terrel...gives eldest son James Reeve remainder of land...provides for daughter Harmony Reeve unmarried...executors: wife Anna Reeve and sons James and John Reeve...witnesses: David Corwin, Asa Corwin, Sally Wichkham. Proved 24 Dec. 1789 by David Corwin and Sally Wickham "spinster". Administration granted 24 Dec. 1789 to Anna Reeve, James and John Reeve.

A-143. STEPHEN REEVE, of Southold, 9 July 1789 ...gives nephew John Reeve land at Shinnecock, at Longsprings, and land bought of Jonah Howel...gives David Reeve remainder of land. . gives friend Elizabeth Smith 20 pounds and other items...executors: John Reeve and William Herrick...witnesses: Hugh Gelston, Abraham Sayre, Stephen Bishop. Proved 25 Dec. 1789 by Hugh Gelston and Abraham Sayre "blacksmith". Administration granted 25 Dec. 1789 to John Reeve and William Herrick.

A-145. ELIAS HOWELL, of Southampton, 22 Jan. l874...gives son Elias Howell land adjoining that of Joshua Sayre and Widow Jagger...gives daughter Mary Hudson five shillings...gives daughter Hannah Halsey five shillings...gives daughter Abigail Howell 20 pounds...gives daughter Ruth Howell 80 pounds and articles...executors: son Elias Howell and friend Caleb Cooper...witnesses; Joshua Sayre, Elias Peirson, John Post Jr...Proved 26 Dec. 1789 by Joshua Sayre and John Post Jr. Administration granted 26 Dec. 1789 to son Elias Howell.

A-147. DANIEL LOPER, of Easthampton,"laborer", 5 June 1789...gives wife Mary all property..."I expect to leave six children"...wife is sole executrix ...at her death the estate goes to son Joel..."and that he be kind" to his sisters Mercy and Cloe who are to have a home with him until they are married...when wife dies the executor is to be friend Nathaniel Dominy...Codicil with same date and same witnessees: David Talmage Jr.,Eunice Case, Nathaniel Dominy. Proved 31 Dec. 1789 by David Talmage Jr."blacksmith", Eunice Case "spinster", and Nathaniel Dominy "clockmaker." Administration granted 31 Dec. 1789 to widow Mary Loper.

A-149. JACOB PLATT, of Huntington, 10 Dec. 1789...,gives to nephew Joseph Platt, to Joseph's son Jacob Platt, and to Jacob Rogers' two daughters Mary and Experience Rogers...executors: Thomas Ireland, Ephraim Oakes...witnesses: Daniel Higbie, Platt Akerly, Nathaniel Higbie. Proved 7 Jan. 1790 by Platt Akerly Huntington, "mariner". Administration granted 7 Jan. 1790 to Thomas Ireland and Ephraim Oakes.

A-152. JESSE CONKLINE, of Half Hollow Hills, Huntington, 19 Aug. 1789...provides for wife Azubah Conkline...gives daughter Ruth Dingy for life lands at Half Neck...gives son Jesse Conkline remainder of lands...executors: friends Wilmot Oakly and John Oakley...signed COKLIN...witnesses: John Snedecor, John Everitt, Ruth Wood. Proved 7 Dec. 1789 by Ruth Wood, widow, of Huntington. Administration granted 23 Jan. 1790 to Wilmot and John Oakley.

A-154. HUMPHREY AVERY, of Brookhaven, 9 Sept. 1789...gives eldest son Thomas Avery half estate at Pine Neck...gives second son Humphrey Avery all lands at Blue Point...gives third son Nathan Avery, "who is at present time in a state of lunacy" five pounds when he comes to right mind...gives fourth son Roger Avery half lands at Pine Neck...gives eldest daughter Mary Avery 100 pounds..gives second daughter Susanna Avery 120 pounds when married...gives three sons Thomas, Humphrey and Rogers lands in Winthrop's Patent...executors: friend Selah Strong and three sons Thomas, Humphrey and Roger Avery...signed HUMPHREY

AVERY...witnesses: David Rose, Solomon Avery, Zebulon Furman. Proved 29 Jan. 1790 by Zebulon Furman "cordwainer." Administration granted 3 Feb. 1790 to Thomas, Humphrey and Roger Avery.

A-156. DORCUS HENDRICKSON, of Huntington. 30 May 1787...gives to granddaughter Dorcus Smith, granddaughter Mary Ketcham, two daughters Rhoda and Jerusha, and Jerusha's daughter Anna Brown the property bewteen them...executrixes: daughters Rhoda and Jerusha...witnesses: Nathaniel Bunce, Sarah Roger.. Proved 30 Oct.1789 by Nathaniel Bunce "cordwainer" and Sarah Roger "spinster." Administration granted Nathaniel Bunce 5 Feb. 1790, and mentions an instrument dated 30 Oct. 1789 wherein Rhoda Bryan and Jerusha Ruland, relinquish their executrixship.

A-157. JONAH SMITH, of Brookhaven, 20 Oct. 1789...give wife Survillah Smith use of property...makes daughter Joanna Smith heiress...executors: wife Survilah Smith and John Akerly...witnesses: Elisha Hammond, Isaac Hulse. Proved 28 Jan. 1790 by Elisha Hammond 'cordwainer". Administration granted 28 Jan. 1790 to Survilah Smith and John Akerly.

A-159 EZEKIEL HEDGES, of South Haven, 18 Oct. 1782...provides for wife Elizabeth Hedges ... gives two sons Elias and Joseph Hedges whole estate equally divided, Joseph the younger not to have his share until 21...gives three grandsons Abel, Jeremiah and Stephen Swesy 20 pounds each when 21...gives two granddaughters Elizabeth and Jerish Hedges 20 pounds each when 18 or married...executors: wife Elizabeth Hedges and sons Elias and Joseph Hedges...witnesses: Isaac Willets, William Smith, Joseph Hedges. Proved 12 Feb. 1790 by Isaac Willets of New York City. Administration granted 16 Feb. 1790 to Elizabeth Hedges and Elias and Joseph Hedges.

A-160. JOHN JAYNE, of South Mills, Jan. 1781...provides for wife Mary Jayne... also for brother Micah Jayne...executors: wife Mary and brother Micah Jayne...wife signed with testator...witnesses: William Booth, Ruth Smith, Hannah Smith.

Proved 28 Jan. 1790 by Hannah Smith "spinster". Administration granted 29 Mar. 1790 to Mary Jayne.

A-162. JAMES LOPER, of Easthampton, 4 May 1785...gives wife Mary property use... remembers son Daniel...gives son Amus lands formerly of Capt. Elias Hand...gives sons James, William and Abraham five shillings each...gives granddaughter Phebe five shillings...gives lands in Montauk and Hapeague to three grandsons Jeremy, Daniel and Hinry, all under 21, sons of son Abraham...executors; wife Mary and Isaac Edwards... witnesses: Nathaniel Hand. Nathan Miller, Elizabeth Hand. Proved 2 Apr. 1790 by Nathaniel Hand. Administration granted 6 Apr.1790 to Isaac Edwards.

A-164. SAMUEL HUTCHINSON, of Easthampton, physician, 21 Feb. 1790...gives wife Hannah land bought of Nathan Conkling...mentions possibility of sons marrying... gives two eldest sons Samuel and Henry land formerly their grandfather Parsons, also land at Aquebonock and Montauk...gives youngest son Ely land bought of Jeremiah Conklin and Abraham Edwards, also dead against David Leek, a deed and bond from Robert Parsons, land at Long Hollow...gives youngest daughter Elizabeth 100 pounds... gives grandson Samuel Conkling, son of Daniel Conkling, remembrance...gives son Samuel rights to Clinton Academy ...mentions daughter Elizabeth and her sister Phebe, tombstones for late father Parsons, wife Phebe and son John, all three deceased, and himself...gives daughter Mary Mulford five shillings...mentions wife Hannah, and daughters Hannah, Mehitabel, Phebe and Elizabeth... executors: son Samuel, son-in-law Daniel Conkling, and kinsman Nathaniel Dominy... witnesses: Ebenezer Sage, Jonathan Mulford, Constant Booth. Proved 3 Apr. 1790 by Ebenezer Sage, "physician" and Jonathan Mulford . Administration granted 6 Apr. 1790 to Samuel Hutchinson and Daniel Conkling.

A-167. CAPT. THOMAS CONKLING, of Brig. Gen. De Lancies 1st Batt. verbally, "dav before he died"...third of estate to sister...third of estate to cousin Rebekkah Conklin of Huntington...third of estate to Thomas Squires, son of John Squires of Huntington...according to affidavit signed by Lt.

Nehemiah Rogers,25, of the same battalion 14 Mar. 1782 before Angus Campbell, Notary Public and Justice of the Peace, with witnesses: Thomas Wright and John Early, at Charles-town, South Carolina, whereby will was proved. Administration granted 8 Apr.1790 to Adam Lefford.

A-169. RHODA BRYAN, of Huntington, relict of Epenetus Bryan, 30 Oct. 1789...gives grandson Charles Grice a note of five pounds against Jacob Bryan...all else divided between daughter Jemima and son Azel... executors: Whitehead Guildersleeve and Thomas Ireland...witnesses: Thomas Tredwell, Nathaniel Bunce, Sarah Rogers...Proved 14 Dec. 1789 by Nathaniel Bunce "cordwainer" and Sarah Rogers "widow". Administration granted 8 Apr. 1790 to Jemima Sell, Whitehead Guildersleeve and Thomas Ireland having relinquished executorship on 5 Feb.1790 and 13 Mar. 1790.

A-172. PHEBE SAMMIS, of Huntington, widow of John Sammis...11 Aug. 1787... given portions to four children, John and Selah Platt, Phebe Wheeler and Elizabeth Raiment...gives portion to children of daughter Mary Wickes, deceased...gives two grandchildren, Philip Plat and Mary Sammis a portion of dower due from estate of former husband Philip Platt, deceased...executors; Ananias Conkling and Jacamiah Brush...witnesses: Richard Brown, Reuben Johnson, John Ketcham. Proved 8 Apr. 1790 by Reuben Brown, "cooper," and John Ketcham. Administration granted 10 Apr. 1790 to Ananias Conkling and Jacamiah Brush.

A-174. ELKANA CONKLINE, of Huntington... I June 1787...gives son John Carman Conkline mare bought of Samuel Wood...gives eldest daughter Hannah Hendrickson 100 pounds...gives daughter Mary Conkline 200 pounds and furniture...to wife Mary five pounds....gives two sons Epenetus and Elkana estate in common when 21 or married... executors: Epenetus Conkline and Jacob Conkline, brothers... witnesses: Micah Hartt, Jesse Platt, Platt Conkline. Proved 8 Apr. 1790 by Micah Hartt. Administration granted 12 May 1790 to Epenetus and Elkana Conkline.

A-176. EZEKIEL SANFORD, of Southampton,..18 June 1789...gives wife Sarah Sandford 20 pounds...gives daughter Mehitabel Hill 20 pounds and "chest which was her mothers..."...gives daughter Achsah Griswold eight pounds...daughters Elizabeth Carpenter, Phebe Parmelee, Mary Halsey and Caroline Cook all have their portions... gives son Benjamin Sandford land at Sag Harbor, adjoining land of Thomas Cooper and Elias Sandford...gives son Bethuel Sandford land adjoining that of David Sandford...gives son Ezekiel Sandford the residue of land... executors: son Ezekiel Sandford, John Cook... witnesses: David Howell, Josiah Sandford, Hezekiel Sandford. Proved 26 July 1790 by David Howell the III. Administration granted 10 Aug. 1790 to Ezekiel Sandford.

A-178. THOMAS REEVE, of Southold, 15 May 1789...provides for wife Kezia Reeve ...gives two daughters Sarah and Experience as much as other two daughters have had... remainder given equally to four daughters Kezia, Hannah, Sarah, Experience...gives son Thomas Reeve land...he to pay son Daniel 50 pounds...gives son James a gift... gives son Barnabas 18 pounds...gives son Daniel land in Mattatick and rights in Dayton Manor...remembers son John...executors: wife Kezia Reeve and two sons Thomas and John...witnesses: John Hubbard, Joseph Corwin, Amaziah Corwin. Proved 29 July 1790 by John Hubbard, "merchant," and Joseph and Amziah Corwin. Administration granted 11 Aug. 1790 to Kezia Reeve and Thomas and John Reeve.

A-180. BENJAMIN SMITH, of Brookhaven, 19 May 1790... gives two sons James and Israel lands equally divided...they to educate and bring up grandson William Smith, son of Benjamin Smith, deceased, and put him to a trade...gives son Samuel and daughter Freelove 30 pounds each, provided Mr. Nicoll's survey is according to expectation... executors: sons James and Iarael, and John Akerly...witnesses: Daniel Saxton, John Saxton, Jeremiah Goldsmith. Proved 16 Aug. 1790 by Daniel and John Saxton "cordwainers" of Brookhavon. Administration granted 30 Aug. 1790 to James and Israel Smith and John Akerly.

26

A-182. DAVID GARDINER, of Isle of Wight at Easthampton, 7 Sept. 1774. ..gives wife Jerusha Gardiner 350 pounds and half use of land for life...gives sister Jerusha Gardiner 100 pounds...gives brother Septimus Gardiner 40 pounds...gives sister Hannah Gardiner 25 pounds... gives youngest son David Gardiner lands in New London, Conn...gives oldest son John Lyon Gardiner lands in Isle of Wight or Gardiner's Island...executors: two uncles Coll. Abraham Gardiner and Captain David Mulford, and friend Thomas Wickham are also guardians instructed to bring up children until of age...witnesses: John Chatfield, Sineus Dibbel, Abraham Miller. Proved 16 Sept.1774 before Maltby Gelston by John Chatfield, Abraham Miller "merchant," and Sineus Dibbel. Administration granted 6 Oct. 1774 by Cadwallader Colden, Lieut. Gov. and Comm. in Chief of Province of New York, to Abraham Gardiner, David Mulford and Thomas Wickham. Sam Bayard Jr. certifies to copy of will. New administration granted 27 Aug.1790 to Nathaniel Gardiner and David Mulford, nephews of David Gardiner, by Surrogate Thomas Tredwell, it being noted that Thomas Wickham "last surviving of aforesaid executors" lately died interstate.

A-186. EZEKIEL HEDGES, of Brookhaven, 1 Oct. 1782...gives wife Hannah Hedges 100 pounds...gives two daughters Elizabetth Hedges and Jerusha Hedges affects of first wife, Joanna Hedges, their mother...executors: William Swezey and Stephen Swezey...witnesses: Jacob Green, Thaddeus Cole, Elias Hedges. Proved 30 Aug. 1790, by Thaddeus Cole of Brookhaven. Administration granted 8 Sept. 1790 to William and Stephen Swezey.

A-187. NATHANIEL WOODRUFF, of Brookhaven, 27 Mar. 1787...gives son Matthew Woodruff land in Yaphank Neck, land bought of Richard Woodhull and of Micah Mills at South Haven and Southampton...gives eldest son James Woodruff five shillings ...gives grandson Jonathan Jones five shillings...gives each of Ebenezer Homan's children by daughter Anna five shillings when of age...executor: Matthew Woodruff...witnesses: Henry Hulse, Esther Rose, David Rose. Proved 6 Sept. 1790 by Henry Hulse and David Rose "clerk" of Brookhaven. Administration granted 10 Sept.1790 to son Matthew Woodruff.

A-189 . TIMOTHY WELLS, of Southold, 22 Dec. 1789.. provides for wife Mary Wells ... gives son John Wells half estate when 21...gives two daughters Mary and Martha Woodruff quarter estate each when 18 or married...executors to be guardians of three children...executors: father-in-law John Wells, and uncle Manly Wells...witnesses: Lion Gardiner, Benjamin Penny, Luther Gardiner. Proved 28 July 1790 by Lion Gardiner of Southold, "blacksmith". Administration granted 24 Sept.1790 to John Wells and Manly Wells.

A-191. DANIEL TERRY, oF Southold, 9 Aug. 1787...provides for wife Mary...gives son James Terry land at South Harbor...gives son William Terry land...gives three daughters Mary, Louisa and Abigail room and garden...gives son Daniel Terry five shillings...executors: friend James Tuthill, and son James Terry...witnesses: Benjamin Davis, Joshua Salmon Jr., James W. Booth... Proved 5 Oct. 1790 by James Wheelock Booth of Southold. Administration granted 5 Oct. 1790 to James Terry.

A-192. SIMON FLEET, of Huntington, 12 June 1790...gives wife Deborah Fleet provisions...gives daughter Rebekah and daughter Ann gifts ...gives daughter Sarah a negress Rose...gives son John a negro boy Bill...gives son Alexander a negro Jim and land adjoining that of Gilbert Fleet and Timothy Scudder, and land in Crabmeadow...gives son John remaining land... executors: son Alexander Fleet and John Stratton... witnesses: Henry Scudder, Joseph Skillman, Isaac Buffet. Proved 4 Aug.1790 by Joseph Skillman of Huntington, and 5 Aug. 1790 by Isaac Buffet of Smithtown. Administration granted 26 Oct. 1790 to Alexander Fleet and John Stratton.

A-195. JOHN FLEET, of Huntington, 24 Sept. l790...provides for wife... mentions will and debts of father...all land to son Joshua, with his care and education in hands of his mother...executors: Alexander Fleet and John Stratton... witnesses: Henry Scudder, Ransler Fleet, Gilbert Akly. Proved 25 Oct. 1790 by Henry Scudder of Huntington. Administration granted 12 Nov. 1790 to Alexander Fleet and John Stratton.

A-196, JOSHUA CLEVES, of Southold, 3 Nov. 1790... gives wife Mehetable 10 pounds and provisions... gives eldest son Jonathan five shillings... gives second son Daniel all lands. ..gives son Daniel and four daughters Experience, Phebe, Mary, and Jemima moveables equally divided... executors: friends John C. Terry and David Conkling... witnesses: David Conkling, James Moore, David Warner. Proved 23 Nov.1790 by David Conkling "physician," James Moore and David Warner, all of Southold. Administration granted 27 Nov. 1790 to John C. Terry and David Conkling.

A-198. SAMUEL PARSONS, of Easthampton, 23 Aug 1790...provides for wife...gives son Merry land adjoining that of Robert Parsons, and share in Montauk... gives son Samuel land bought of John Huntting, and dwelling house, except half given wife and four daughters Mary, Puah, Jemimah and Hannah while single...gives son Eli land adjoining that of John Parsons and Henry Doininies Hands...three sons to pay their four sisters 30 pounds each... executors: wife Mary Parsons and three sons: Merrey, Samuel and Eli Parsons...witnesses: Jesse Dayton, Jonathan Tuthill and John Stratton. Proved 20 Dec. 1790 by Jesse Davton "hatter," and John Stratton "schoolmaster," both of Easthampton. Administration granted 24 Dec.1790, to three sons Merrey, Samuel and Eli Parsons.

A-200. JACKSON SCOTT, of Southampton, 23 Apr. 1790... provides for wife... gives daughter Deborah 25 pounds and land and home while single...gives three daughters Mary, Temperance and Sarah six shillings each... gives son Matthew Scott land in Jeffery's Neck and Cow Neck, also land adjoining that of John Haines... gives son Thomas Scott 15 pounds... executors to sell land adjoining that of heirs of Thomas Jinnings, and heirs of Christopher Lapton... gives two sons Jackson Scott and Samuel Scott land adjoining Silvanus Jinnings... executors: two friends Caleb Cooper and Captain Abraham Sayre... witnesses: Zebulon Jessup, Susan Hallsey, Silas Halsey. Proved 22 Dec. 1790 by Zebulon Jessup "tanner," and Silas Halsey, both of Southampton. Administration granted 25 Dec. 1790 to Caleb Cooper and Abraham Sayre.

A-203. ISAAC SMITH, of Dicks Hills in Huntington, 4 Mar. 1779... provides for wife Sarah Smith... gives three sons Isaac, Jesse and Jacob stock and 50 pounds each... remembers two daughters Sarah Buffet and Elizabeth Carmon... gives Zebulon Smith, son, land... executors: two sons Zebulon and Jesse Smith... witnesses: Conkling Ketcham, John Ketcham, Solomon Ketcham. Proved 28 Jan. 1791 by John Ketcham of Huntington. Administration granted 31 Jan. 1791 to Zebulon Smith.

A-205. WILLIAM SAMMIS, of Huntington, 26 May 1790...executors to sell land bought of James Long between West Neck and Huntington ... provides for wife Sarah Sammis, who will get certain stock after his father's decease... gives sons William and Jarvis Sammis lands equally divided... daughters Susannah, Mary, Sarah, Ruth, Hannah, Deborah, Phebe, Olly Sammis to have home while single... gives daughter Susannah 25 pounds and other daughters 20 pounds...executors to give sons William and Jarvis schooling, and a trade at 15... executors: friends Jacamiah Brush, Richard Conkling... witnesses: Selah Conkling, Augustain Sammis, John Sammis. Proved 28 Jan. 1791 by Selah Conkling, "weaver" of Huntington. Administration granted 1 Feb. 1791 to Jacamiah Brush and Richard Conkling.

A-206. AMBROUS WICKS, of Huntington, 10 May 1787...provides for wife Phebe ... gives son Azariah Wicks land...gives son Jones Wicks five shillings... gives son David Wicks five shillings...gives daughter Kesiah Vail five shillings... gives dauahter Charity Wicks five shillings, ... give daughter Persiller [Priscilla] a heifer... gives daughter Mary Wicks five shillings...executors: friends Epenetus Conkling, Eliphalet Jervis and Phebe Wicks, all of Huntington ... witnesses: William Lysaght, Eliphalet Jervis. Proved 28 Jan. 1791 by William Lysaght "ship carpenter," and Eliphalet Jervis, both of Huntington ...naming testator Ambrose. "Meramion" codicil 12 May 1787 gives two horses to Azeriah Wicks... same witnesses. Proved 28 Jan. 1791 by same witnesses. Administration granted 2 Feb. 1791 to Eliphalet Jervis.

A-208. MATTHEW WOODRUFF, of Brookhaven, 8 Feb. 1791...
provides for wife Ablgail Woodruff... gives eldest son Nathaniel
Woodruff farm "my father Nathaniel Woodruff" bought of Micah
Mills...gives second and third sons Jehiel and Jesse Woodruff,
divided equally, lands at Yaphank Neck, Fireplace Neck bought
of Richard Woodhull... lands at Southampton to be sold and
proceeds given three daughters Phebe, Elizabeth and Mary
Woodruff at 18... executors: Rev. David Rose, Isaac Overton
and Capt. William Phillips... witnesses: Daniel Robert, Isaiah
Reeve, Mordecai Homan. Proved 11 Feb. 1791 by Daniel Robert
:physician," Isaiah Reeve "weaver," and Mordecai Homan
"cordwainer," all of Brookhaven. Administration granted 11 Feb.
1791 to David Rose, Isaac Overton and William Phillips.

A-210. OBADIAH JOHNES, of Huntington, 25 Nov. 1789... gives
son Gardiner Johnes 20 pounds... gives son Thomas Johnes 20
pounds... gives daughter Mary Rogers 20 pounds... gives son
William Johnes remainder of estate in Southampton... executor:
son William Johnes... witnesses: Joseph Wickes, Jacob
Scudder, Obadiah Wickes. Proved 5 Mar. 1791 by Joseph and
Obadiah Wickes "cooper" of Huntington. Administration granted
10 Mar. 1791 to son William Johnes.

A-211. JOHN MILLER, of Easthampton, 8 Nov. 1784... provides for
wife Rebekah... gives son Lewis Miller five pounds... gives three
grandsons, sons of late son Daniel, Zadok, and Lewis five shillings
each...gives grandson John Miller, son of late son Daniel, 100 pounds
at 21... gives son John Miller reminder of estate on condition he bring
up grandchildren ... executors: wife Rebekah, son John Miller and
friend John Chatfield... witnesses: John Chatfield, Henry Chatfield,
Huntting Miller. Proved 16 Apr. 1791 by John Chatfield, Henry
Chatfield, Huntting Miller, all of Easthampton. Administraticn
granted 16 Apr. 1791 to Rebekah Miller and John Miller.

A-213. JOB SMITH, of Smithtown, 5 Oct. 1787... gives brother
Nicolas Smith whole estate... "excutors: brother Nicolas Smith
and uncle Epenetus Smith... witnesses: Moses Smith, John
Smith, Mary Smith. Proved 15 Apr. 1791 by John Smith.
Administration granted 18 Apr. 1791 to Nicholas Smith.

A-214. JAMES YOUNGS, of Southold, 1 Nov.1790...gives son James Youngs land at Broad Meadows... gives wife Mehetabal Youngs 100 pounds... gives daughter Abigail Wells half Roan Oak Farm adjoining land of Thomas Youngs, Manly Wells and Daniel Terrey... gives two grandchildren James Wells and Mehetabel Wells, children of Manly Wells and "my daughter" Joanne Wells, deceased, the other half of Roan Oak Farm... son Abraham Youngs to be supported by estate... executors: son James Youngs, son-in-law David Wells and son-in-law Manly Wells... witnesses: HenryTerry, Paul Reeve Jr., Daniel Wells. Proved 18 Apr. 1791 by Henry Terry and Daniel Wells, both of Southold. Administration granted 20 Apr. 1791 to James Youngs, David and Manly Wells.

A-216. PETER DOWNS, of Southold, 30 Nov. 1790... wills everything to wife Mary Downs and for support of son Peter Downss... executrix: wife Mary Downs...witneesses: Jeremiah Corwin, Henry Corwin, Daniel Wells. Proved 18 Apr. 1791 by Jere Corwin "carpenter" and Daniel Wells, both of Southold. Aministration granted 21 Apr. 1791 to Mary Downs.

A-217. JAMES LYONS, of Brookhaven, (an unrecorded will on file dated 29 May 1789 mentions daughter Anne Lyons to have 300 pounds and apparel of wife and daughter late deceased... nephew Thomas Lyons, son of brother John Lyons, living near Verner's old tavern eight miles this side of Lancaster, Pa... and brother Joseph Lyons who lived at Donnegal... executors: friends Abraham Woodhull, Thomas Helme and Joseph Brewster, and nephew Thomas Lyons, also Philetus Smith ... witnesses: Amos Smith, George Muirson Punderson, John Curtis, Charles Dallas.) [recorded will] "very far advanced in years"...29 May 1790... gives brother Thomas Lyons 350 pounnds, with nephew Thomas Lyons to inherit if he take brother to live with him in Pennsylvania... gives dauughter Anne Lyons 900 pounds and apparel of wife and daughter deceased... gives nephew Thomas Lyons of Penns. two thirds of estate... gives children of brother Joseph Lyons third of estate to be handled by Thomas Lyons of Penns. ... executors: friends Thomas Helme, Philetus Smith, Joseph Brewster, Amos Smith, Sr., and nephew Thomas Lyons... signed Lyon... witnesses: Cornelius Clark,

Amos Smith, John Curtis. Proved 12 May 1791 by Cornelius Clark "mariner," and John Curtis "schoolmaster," both of Brookhaven. Administration granted 14 May 1791 to Thomas Helme, Philetus Smith and Thomas Lyons.

A-219. ISRAEL WOOD, of Huntington, 6 May 1791...estate to be sold... gives wife a servant girl Phillis and 200 Dounds...remainder of money to be equally divided among children, Experience Peck, daughter, to receive portion at 21... executors: Samuel Wood, Zophar Platt Jr., and David Rusco Jr... witnesses: Carll Ketcham, Joseph Lewis, Ebenezer Platt. Proved 9 May 1791 by Carll Ketcham, Joseph Lewis, Ebenezer Platt, all of Huntington. Codicil 8 May 1791 provided for daughter Experience Peck... same witnesses. Proved 9 May 1791 by same witnesses. Codicil by slate "whilst he lay ill of a mortal wound, of which he died soon after," to provide bed and furniture for wife... 8 May 1791. Sworn to by witnesses 18 May 1791. Administration granted 19 May 1791 to Samuel Wood, Zophar Platt Jr.,and David Rusco Jr. (Experience Peck approves will in letter 17 May 1791)

A-222. ABRAHAM ROSE, of Southampton, 29 Mar. 1791... gives wife 40 pounds and goods in lieu of dower... gives son Samuel Rose land bought of Abraham Hallsey, Thonas Howell, and land at Canoe Place... gives son Rufus land adjoining that of Samuel Hains, and land bought of Thomas Sandford, John Rogers... gives granddaughter Clarissa Rose 10 pounds... gives son Abraham remainder... executors: wife and two sons Samuel Hains Rose and Abraham Rose... witnesses: Henry Halsey, Henry Ludlow, John Gelston. Proved 27 May 1791 by Henry Halsey and John Gelston, both of Southampton. Administration granted 1 June 1791 to Samuel Hains and Abraham Rose.

A-223. BARNABUS TERREL, of Southold, 16 Apr. 1791... gives daughter Bethiah Wickham land at Fort Neck for life... then gives it to grandchildren David Horton, Sarah Conkling, Bethiah Hubbard, Kesiah Reves and Prudence Horton equally... gives grandson John Hubbard land already using and negro Cain, but "not; to sell him without his consent"... gives daughter Mary Fanning land where grandson Thomas Hubbard now lives...

gives two grandsons John and Thomas Hubbard land... gives Thomas Hubbard 100 pounds... gives two daughters Bethiah Wickham and Mary Fanning remainder... executors: son-in-law, John Wickham and grandson John Hubbard... witnesses: David Conkling, Obadiah Hudson, Matthew Peases. Proved 30 May 1791 by Matthew Peases "cordwainer," of Southold. Administration granted 1June 1791 to John Wickham and John Hubbard.

A-225. JAMES DOWNS, (probably of Southold) 13 May 1784...gives son James Downs whole estate except household goods... if he should die before of age a third of estate is given to oldest child of daughter Hannah Downs, and the remainder to daughter Mehitable Downs who gets household goods at 21... son James is to pay daughter Hannah 20 pounds and daughter Mehitable 150 pounds... executor: Jeremiah Wells... witnesses: Ezekiel Petty, Hannah Wells, Nathaniel Wells. Proved 30 May 1791 by Hannah Wells "spinster" and Nathaniel Wells, both of Southold. Administration granted 2 June 1791 to Jeremiah Wells.

A-227. DANIEL FOSTER, of Southampton,"husbandman," 26 July 1786... gives son David Hains Foster commonage at Canoe Place, a desk and five pounds... gives son Rufus Foster land "left me by my father," to care for "my son Peter...as a tender brother who art acquainted with his infirmities"... gives son Peter Foster land bought of Fithin Halsey... gives wife Temperance Foster provisions... gives daughter Hannah Brewster 60 pounds... gives two daughters Pamela and Jerusha Foster 80 pounds and home while single...gives son Rufus land bought of John Halsey... executors: sons David Hains Foster and Rufus Foster... witnesses: Stephen Jagger, Miriam Jagger, Anna Jagger. Proved 31 May 1791 by Stephen and Miriam Jagger and Ann Jagger "spinster," all of Southampton. Administration granted 3 June 1791 to David Hains and Rufus Foster.

A-229. JOSIAH ROGERS, of Huntington, 5 Sept. 1791... gives wife half of personal estate... gives son Thomas land adjoining that of Joel Rogers, and land at Huntington South... gives son Robert lands bought of Platt Arthur at Clay Pits, a bond against

Van Hackly Robbins... gives two sons Platt and Medad remaining two thirds of land except Melancthon's portion... gives son Melancthon land between Cow Harbor and Dicks Hills, he to pay 50 pounds to executors when 21...gives eldest son William 10 pounds...gives daughter Ruth, wife of Henry Smith Jr., 10 pounds...gives daughter Esther, wife of Scudder Platt, 10 pounds... gives daughter Eelse, wife of Eliphalet Carll, 20 pounds... gives daughter Jerusha, wife of Thomas Skillman 20 pounds... gives daughter Experience 40 pounds... gives daughter Rachel 40 pounds... gives Corp. of Presby. Congr. of Huntington 15 pounds left by father Thomas Rogers... son Melancthon to have a trade... executors: Ebenezer Platt, Henry Scudder Lewis...witnesses: Nathaniel Akerly, John Kelcy, Nathaniel Bunce. Proved 10 Oct. 1791 by John Kelcy of Huntington,"cordwainer." Codicil 8 Sept. 1791 with same witnesses. Proved 10 Oct. 1791 by all witnesses. Administration granted 10 Oct. 1791 to Ebenezer Platt and Henry Scudder Lewis.

A-233. HANNAH SCIDMORE, of Huntington, widow of Joseph Scidmore, 26 Feb. 1788... "laboring under great infirmities"... gives son Isaac whole estate... executor: son Isaac Scidmore... witnesses: Seth Jarvis, Samuel Nichols, Elizabeth Nichols. Proved 11 Oct. 1791 by Seth Jarvis "weaver," and Elizabeth Nichols "spinster," both of Smithtown. Administration granted 11 Oct. 1791 to Isaac Scidmore.

A-235. JOHN HOWELL, of Southampton, 24 May 1791... gives son John Howell land adjoining Thomas Jessup's land at Noyac, Pogenquage and Canoe Place, Quage and Topping... gives son James Howell 40 shillings... gives son Nathan Howell 40 shillings... gives daughter Mary Sayre 20 pounds... gives grandson John Howell five pounds... gives son Stephen Howel land bought of brother Ebenezer... gives granddaughter Jane Sayre a glass... gives granddaughter Lucretia Howel five pounds... executors: two sons John and Stephen Howell...witnesses: Thomas Jessup Jr., Ebenezer Jessup, William Herrick. Proved 6 Oct. 1791 by Thomas Jessup and Ebenezer Jessup "shopjoiner," of Southampton. Administration granted 11 Oct. 1791 to John Howell.

35

A-236. JAMES BISHOP, of Southampton, 10 Oct. 1785...
Marshals Close to be sold... provides for wife Susanah... gives
son Stephen Bishop six shillings... gives son George Bishop all
land... executors: wife Susanah and George Bishop, son, and
friend Jeremiah Post... witnesses: Hannah Goldsmith, Betsey
Goldsmith, Joseph Goldsmith. Proved 6 Oct. 1791 by Joseph
Goldsmith "blacksmith," and Hannah Goldsmith "spinster," both
of Southampton. Administration granted 12 Oct.1791 to
Susanah Bishop, George Bishop and Jeremiah Post.

A-28. WILLIAM FOSTER, of Southampton, farmer, 22 Aug.
1781... gives daughter-in-law Ann Foster privilege to live in
home... gives grandson David Foster 100 pounds... to
granddaughter Sarah Foster a gift... gives two sons Benjamin
Foster, Stephen Foster and grandson William Foster remainder
equally divided... executors: sons Benjamin and Stephen Foster
and grandson William Foster... witnesses; Isaac Post, Josiah
Foster, James Post. Proved 6 Oct. 1791 by James Post of
Southampton. Administration granted 12 Oct. 1791 to Benjamin,
Stephen and William Foster.

A-240. HENRY POST, of Southampton, 17 Oct. 1790... provides
for wife... movables to revert to those of son and two daughters
unmarried when wife dies... gives three daughters Eunice
Pierson, Mercy Hildreth and Hannah Harris five shillings each...
two daughters Deborah and Charity Post to have home until
married or son is 21... gives son Henry Post land... executors:
wife and two brothers Stephen and Jeremiah Post... witnesses:
Stephen Post, Nathan Foster, William Herrick. Proved 6 Oct.
1791 by Stephen Post, Nathan Foster "cooper," and William
Herrick. Administration granted 12 Oct. 1791 to Mrs. Post,
Stephen and Jeremiah Post.

A-241. ELIZABETH GILDERSLEEVE of Huntington, 23 Mar.
1789... "very weak"... gives granddaughter Elizabeth
Gildersleeve, under 18, her mothers clothes ... gives daughters
Rebecca Platt, Mary Hubbard, Ruth Smith, Sarah Rogers,
Deborah Scribmore money to be divided with granddaughter
Elizabeth Gildersleeve... executors: Joseph Platt... witnesses:
Selah Ketcham, Jemima Ketcham. Proved 13 Oct. 1791 by

Selah Ketcham "wheelwright," of Huntington. Administration granted 13 Oct. 1791 to Joseph Platt.

A-243. MOSES ROLPH, of Huntington, 18 Oct. 1791... gives sons Reuben Rolph and Benjamin Rolph land adjoining that of Zophar Platt Jr. and land formerly of Israel Wood, deceased...gives son David Rolph land adjoining that of Zachariah Smith... gives daughter Rebeckah Oakley five pounds... gives daughter Hannah Platt five pounds... executors to sell land formerly of Hubal Smith, Job Sammis, Thomas Wickes, and land adjoining that of Michael Remp, for support of daughter Phebe Rolph... executors: son Reuben Rolph and son-in-law Samuel Oakley... witnesses: David Rusco Jr., Elkanah Cornish, John Ketcham. Proved 10 Jan 1792 by John Ketcham of Huntington. Administration granted 10 Jan 1792 to Reuben Rolph and Samuel Oakley.

A-245. JOHN ROGERS, of Huntington, 19 Mar. 1788... gives wife Ruth Rogers land at Great Neck... gives two eldest daughters Phebe and Mary 50 pounds each... gives two youngest daughters Deborah and Elizabeth 100 pounds each... gives son Zebulon Whitman Rogers 400 pounds... gives two sons John and Jervis Rogers remainder of estate when of age... executors: son John Rogers and friends John Oakley and Jacobus Nostran... wife signed... witnesses: Zachariah Rogers, Esther Dinge, Ebenezer Rogers. Proved 11 Jan. 1792 by Zachariah Rogers. Administration granted 11 Jan. 1792 to John Rogers, John Oakley, Jacobus Nostran.

cA-247. NEHEMIAH WHITMAN, of Huntington, I June 1789... gives wife Phebe Whitman goods, 50 pounds and a negress... gives son Isaac Whitman 15 pounds... gives granddaughter Hannah Phillips five pounds when of age... gives two daughters Ruth Conkline and Phebe Jervis, and eight grandchildren, the children of Sarah Platt, deceased, the moveables -- the grandchildren when of age... gives son Jesse Whitman lands in Little Neck adjoining lands of Israel Carll... gives son Stephen Whitman land... gives son Joseph Whitman land adjoining that of Richard Wiggins, Joseph White, deceased, and Theodorus Van Wikes... gives son Stephen land bought of John Whitman,

37

deceased, in West Hills, and land adjoining that of Samuel Oakley and Robert Jarvis...Stephen is to pay 116 pounds with interest to executors... gives son Jesse Whitman remaining land... executors: friend John Buffet, John Oakley and son Jesse Whitman... witnesses: Nathaniel Whitman Jr., Tredwell Scudder, William T. Oakley. Proved 11 Jan. 1792 by Nathaniel Whitman of Huntington. Administration granted 11 Jan. 1792 to John Buffet, John Oakley, Jesse Whitman.

A-251. NATHANIEL AKERLY, of Brookhaven, I Sept. 1790... gives son Elijah Akerly all lands... gives Doryty, wife of Stephen Akerly, provisions for life, then to granddaughters, the children of daughter Dority... gives other three daughters Ruth, Martha and Charity remainder of property... executors: son-in-law Nathaniel Davis, and Abraham Woodhull... witnesses: Thomas Smith, Caturah Tooker, Nathan Woodhull. Proved 28 Feb. 1792 by Thomas Smith and Nathan Woodhull. Administration granted 28 Feb. 1792 to Nathaniel Davis and Abraham Woodhull.

c A-253. DANIEL MOORE, of Southampton, farmer, 17 Mar. 1791... gives son Daniel 70 pounds... gives son Joseph land...gives daughter Anna Petty 65 pounds... gives daughter Hannah Bigelow 24 pounds... gives daughter Elizabeth Pierson seven pounds... gives daughter Elizabeth's two daughters Elizabeth and Prudence seven pounds each when 18... excess money given to children of my sons Stephen, Silas and David "each male twice as much as each female" when of age... executors: f:riends Capt. David Sayre and Moses Howell... witnesses: Paul Hallsey, Elias Matthews, Stephen Halsey. Proved Mar. 1792 by Elias Matthews. Administration granted 14 Mar. 1792 to David Sayre and Moses Howell.

A-255. JOHN WOODRUFF, of Southampton, 12 Mar. 1792... provides for wife... gives son John lands... gives son Abraham land at Sag Harbor, and adjoining that of Silia Stuward... gives four daughters Sarah, Elizabeth, Rebeacah and Mary remainder of moveables equally divided... executors: Benjamin Woodruff and Jesse Woodruff... witnesses: Isaac Hallsey, Mary Halsey. Proved 27 Mar. 1792 by Isaac Halsey "cordwainer". Administration granted 27 Mar. 1792 to Jesse Woodruff "weaver,"of Southampton.

A-257. THOMAS DERING, of Shelter Island, 24 Jan. 1784...
"being sick"... gives wife Mary Dering provisions... gives two
sons Sylvester Dering and Henry Packer Dering land on Shelter
Island, formerly of Brindley Sylvester, deceased, land on east
side of Connecticut River in New Hampshire and in Pomfret...
gives daughter Elizabeth Dering 500 pounds within 12 years...
executrix: wife Mary Dering... witnesses: Joshua Youngs, Mary
Floyd, Ezra L'Hommedieu. Proved 26 Apr. 1792 by Ezra
L'Hommedieu. Administration granted 26 Apr. 1792 to Mary
Dering.

A-260. ELIAZER HAWKINS, of Brookhaven, 23 Oct. 1788...
gives wife moveables for life, then to divide between two
daughters... gives son Jonas land adjoining that of John Hallock,
William Mills, land "father gave me," and lot bought of Ezekiel
Smith... gives son Eliazer land remaining... executors: wife and
sons Jonas and Ezekiel Hawkins... witnesses: Isaac Davis,
Jonas Davis, William Rudyard. Proved 25 May 1792 by Isaac
Davis of Brookhaven. Administration granted 25 May 1792 to
Jonas Hawkins.

A-261. DAVID WELLS, of Riverhead, I July 1792... gives eldest
son David 10 pounds... estate to be sold... provides for wife
Sarah... rest of money between children, born and unborn, of
present wife, sons to have three parts and daughter or
daughters to have two parts... executors: wife Sarah and Decon
Henry Herrick... witnesses: David Conkling, Nathaniel Wells,
John Wells. Proved 17 Sept. 1792 by David Conkling
"physician." Administration granted 17 Sept. 1792 to Sarah
Wells.

cA-263. WILLIAM JONES, of Southampton, 9 Oct. 1776... gives
wife Mary Jones use of half land, if she marry to have instead 50
pounds... provides for wife's possible second widowhood... gives
daughter-in-law Hannah Jones, relict of Paul Jones, lately
deceased, use of other half of lands, if she remarry she to have
instead 60 pounds and to take her daughter Elisabeth... gives
grandson Elias Jones land at Canoe Place... gives grandson
William Jones land adjoining that of John Sayre, William Foster,
Donijah Rayner... in case of death of these granddaughter

39

Elizabeth Jones inherits... gives granddaughter Elizabeth Jones 60 pounds at 2... gives daughter Hannah Floyd five shillings... gives daughter Phebel Howell five shillings... executors: wife Mary Jones and friend Caleb Cooper... witnesses: Jonathan Hallsey, Zophar Cooper, Abigail Cooper Jr. Proved 19 Sept. 1792 by Zophar Cooper.

A-265. TIMOTHY CORWIN, of Southold, 16 Dec. 1791... gives wife Mary use of estate... gives two sons Timothy and Amaziah furniture... gives daughter Sarah five pounds... gives three sons Thomas,Timothy and Amaziah estate equally divided, "but in case the child sworn to my son Amaziah should be chargable to my estate" it be deducted from his dividend... executors: wife Mary and two sons Thomas and Timothv... witnesses: David Conkling, John, Clark, Nathaniel Griffing. Proved 3 Oct. 1792 by David Conkling "physician." Administration granted 3 Oct. 1792 to Mary Corwin and Timothy Corwin.

A-267. JOHN KING, of Southold, 15 Feb. 1791... gives wife Phebe King 30 pounds, or three pounds yearly, to be paid by sons John and Rufus equally... gives son John King house, he to pay Rufus 20 pounds... gives sons John and Rufus all land in Oyster Ponds... gives two sons Gilbert and Joseph two thirds, and two daughters Abigail and Mehitable one third of the residue... executors: brother Nathaniel King and brother-in-law Calvin More... witnesses: David Tuthill, Nathaniel Tuthill, Abraham Tuthill. Proved 4 Oct. 1792 by Nathaniel and Abraham Tuthill. Administration granted 4 Oct. 1792 to Nathaniel King and Calvin More.

A-269. HUGH SMITH, of Brookhaven, 10 June 1791... gives wife Anne Smith best negress and provisions... gives son Nicoll Smith land in New Jersey, negress Sib and negroes Ben and David... gives son Josiah Smith land in Meriches patent, Smith Beach on Long Point, and negroes George and Titus... gives son Charles Smith land at Southampton and negro Sam... gives son William Smith land in Meriches Island... gives son Nathaniel Smith land in Southold, negress Hagar and negroes George and Archibald... gives Sarah Hallsey, "young woman who now lives with me", 50 pounds and negress Doll... executors: wife Ann

Smith,sons Nicoll and Josiah Smith, and friends John and Thomas Gelston... witnesses: Henry Corwithy, Hugh Gelston Jr.,Polly Green. Proved 17 Oct. 1792 by Hugh Gelston Jr., "merchant." Administration granted 17 Oct. 1792 to Thomas Gelston and Nicoll Smith.

A-272. ISAIAH WELLS, of Southold, 23 May 1791... gives eldest son Isaiah Wells land... gives second son Elijah Wells land adjoining that of Elisha Wells, father Daniel Wells... gives daughter Mary when 18 remainder of personal estate when wife has taken what is needed for bringing up of family... executors: father Daniel Wells, father-in-law Daniel Terry, and brother-in-law Daniel Terry Jr...witnesses: Isaiah Tuthill, Daniel Shaw and Mehitable King. Proved 30 Oct. 1792 by Isaiah Tuthill and Daniel Shaw of Riverhead. Administration granted 30 Oct. 1792 to Daniel Wells and Daniel Terry Jr.

cA-273. ZOPHAR PLATT, of Huntington, surgeon, 8 Nov. 1790... gives son Jeremiah Platt 300 pounds... gives son Ebenezer Platt land... gives eight children of daughter Phebe Broome (Betsy, Samuel Platt, Henrietta, Mary Platt, Jennet, George Washington, Horatio Gates and Caroline Broome) 300 pounds equally divided... gives five children of daughter Elizabeth Phenix, deceased, (Elizabeth, Alexander, Sidney, Rebecca and Jennet Phenix) 300 pounds equally divided... gives four children of daughter Sarah Ogden, deceased, (Betsy. Robert, Mary and Sarah Ogden) 300 pounds equally divided... gives daughter Hannah Ogden 300 pounds... executors: son Jeremiah Platt, sons-in-law Samuel Broome, Daniel Phenix, Robert Ogden and son Ebenezer Platt ... witnesses: Phillip Conkling, Hubbard Conkling, John Ketcham. Proved 28 Nov. 1792 by John Ketcham. Administration granted 28 Nov. 1792 to Ebenezer Platt.

A-276. JEREMIAH TERRY, of Easthampton, 11 Jan. 1792... provides for wife... gives eldest daughter Mehitable 50 pounds... gives second daughter Anna 50 pounds... gives third daughter (now living) Martha 50 pounds... gives fourth daughter Abigail 50 pounds... all to have home until married... gives eldest son John a quarter of land in Easthampton and quarter in Southold... gives

41

second son Jeremiah quarter of land... gives third son James quarter of land... gives fourth son Samuel quarter of land... executors: wife, son John and friend Henry Domini... witnesses: Elnathan Parsons, Stephen Parsons, Eli Parsons. Proved 15 Mar. 1793 by Stephen and Eli Parsons. Administration granted 15 Mar. 1793 to John Tarry.

A-278. ANTHONY HAINS, of Southampton, 16 Nov. 1792... provides for wife... gives "oldest son lawfully begotten of my son Benjamin" all lands, but in case of Benjamin dying without heirs the estate goes to the oldest son of son Job, and in case Job dies without heirs the estate goes to the oldest son of son John... gives son John six shillings...gives son Job six shillings... gives three daughters Pewer, Temperence and Caroline residue of moveables... executors: wife and son Benjamin Hains... witnesses: Silas Halsey, David Harris, Henry Harris. Proved 15 Mar. 1793 by Silas Halsey "physician." Administration granted 15 Mar.1793 to Benjamin Hains.

A-280. ELEAZER LUCE, of Riverhead, 3 Feb. 1793... executors to sell land adjoining that of Christopher Youngs... provides for wife Mehetabal ... gives sons David and Eleazer land equally divided... gives daughters Mehetabel and Elizabeth 50 pounds each when 18 or married... executors: wife Mahitabel, brother Abraham Luce and brother-in-law David Downs... witnesses: David Conkling, Timothy Reeve, James Reeve. Proved 27 Mar. 1793 by David Conkling "physician." Administration granted 27 Mar. 1793 to Mahitabel Luce, Abraham Luce, David Downs.

A-281. JONATHAN HOWELL Jr., of Southold, 25 Aug. 1791... gives eldest son Jonathan land... gives daughter Cynthia 20 pounds and her mother's clothes... gives sons Jonathan and David bedding... executor: brother John Howell... witnesses: Joseph Parker Wickham, Isaac Davis, Jonathan Horton. Proved 27 Mar. 1793 by Isaac Davis. Administration granted 27 Mar. 1793 to John Howell.

A-282. THOMAS YOUNGS, of Southold, 3 Feb. 1793... provides for wife Rhoda provisions and five pounds yearly... gives son Thomas Youngs quarter of lands... gives son Joshua Youngs quarter of lands... gives son John Youngs quarter of lands (apparently had no children)... gives son Benjamin Youngs quarter of lands (apparently had no children)... executors to sell land in St. George Manor... gives grandchildren 10 pounds each when 21... gives daughters now living Rhoda Brown, Jemima Ayre, Elizabeth Vail and Mary Youngs, and to children of daughter Hannah Rachel, deceased, remainder of estate... gives daughter Mary home until married... gives 40 pounds to sons Thomas and Joshua if they give at least one son a liberal education... executors: sons Thomas, Joshua and John Youngs, and friend Thomas Moore... witnesses: Ezra L'Hommedieu, Joseph Booth, Austin Booth. Codicil gives daughters Mary and Elizabeth (sic) Youngs 20 pounds each. Proved 27 Mar. 1793 by Ezra L'Hommedieu and Joseph Booth "mariner," both of Southold. Administration granted 27 Mar. 1793 to Thomas,Joshua and John Youngs.

A-287. LEMUEL HOWELL, (of Southampton) 19 Apr. 1793... gives John Hulbert half estate... gives sister Mehitable Howell 20 pounds... gives nephew James Fordham 10 pounds... gives brother Ephraim Howell reminder... executors: brother-in-law John Hulbert and brother Ephraim Howell... witnesses: Nathaniel Reeve, Matthew Jessup, Esther Cook. Proved 1May 1793 by Matthew Jessup. Administration granted 1 May 1793 to John Hulbert.

A-289. WILLIAM BREWSTER, of Brookhaven, 15 Jan. 1793... provides for wife Temperence Brewster... gives son Benjamin Brewster all lands... gives daughter Elizabeth Woodhull 100 pounds... gives daughter Temperance Brewster 150 pounds... executors: son-in-law Isaac Brewster and friend John Smith... witnesses: David Glover, Daniel Swazey, John Leek. Proved 25 May 1793 by Daniel Swazey and John Leek "blacksmith." Administration granted 25 May 1793 to Isaac Brewster and John Smith.

A-290. ISAAC BIGGS, of Brookhaven, 15 Nov. 1792... provides for wife Mary... gives son Isaac Smith Biggs all lands... gives daughter Mary, wife of Morris Jayne, 60 pounds and negress Fillis... gives daughter Ruth Biggs 60 pounds and home while single... in case of Isaac Smith Bigg's decease without heir estate to go to daughter Ruth Brewster and daughter Mary's second son Isaac Jayne equally... and provided son Isaac Smith Brewster lose his reason again executors to take charge of estate... executors: Selah Strong, Abraham Woodhull and Amos Smith ... witnesses: Daniel Saterly, Thomas Hawkins, Amos Smith Jr. Proved 29 May 1793 by Daniel Saterly and Amos Smith Jr. Administration granted 29 May 1793 to Abraham Woodhull and Amos Smith.

A-293. MATTHEW BUNCE, of Huntington, 18 May 1791... gives wife Sarah Bunce 30 pounds and goods... gives friend John Close 50 pounds... gives Lemuel Bunce's son Matthew Bunce 20 pounds... gives Dr. Daniel Wiggin's son Matthew Bunce Wiggin 20 pounds... gives Joshua Bunce 30 pounds... gives John Pedrie 30 pounds... gives sister Hannah Smith 10 pounds... gives negro Elijah freedom... gives mulatto Charles a trade and freedom at 21... gives negreas Rhoda freedom when wife dies.. gives sisters Susannah Darow and Hannah Smith, and the daughters Abigail and Hannah of brother George Bunce the residue ... executors: friends Zophar Platt Jr., John Ketcham... witnesses: Selah Conkling, James Kennedy, John Wilson. Proved 12 June 1793 by Selah Conkling. Administration granted 12 June 1793 to Zophar Platt Jr. and John Ketcham.

A-295. NOAH ROGERS, of Huntington, farmer, 13 May 1791... gives daughter Ruth Rogers home while single... gives grandson Jonathan Rogers land...gives daughter Ruth Rogers remainder with grandchildren Elizabeth, Joseph, John, Levinah, Seth,Joshua and Epenetus Rogers, children of son Joshua Rogers, deceased... executors: Joseph Platt, Nathaniel Udle... witnesses: Thomas Ireland, Abel Akerly, Rebekah Platt. Proved 12 June 1793 by Abel Akerly. Administration granted 12 June 1793 to Joseph Platt and Nathaniel Udle.

A-296. HENRY WELLS, of Southold, 15 July 1791... gives eldest son Thomas Dickinson Wells land adjoining that of Daniel Edward, Zebulon Hallock, and lands at Fresh Ponds... gives son Obadiah Wells land... gives son Joseph Wells and two daughter Naomi and Hannah other land equally divided... gives three

daughters Elizabeth, Naomi and Hannah household goods...
executors: sons Obadiah and Thomas Dickinson Wells and son-in-law Jonathan Robinson... witnesses: Daniel Edwards, Jonah Glover, Daniel Edwards Jr. Proved 13 July 1793 by Daniel Edwards "taylor." Administration granted 13 July 1793 to Obadiah Wells.

A-298. JOHN PARSONS, of Easthampton, 16 Sept. 1793... gives wife Deborah provisions... gives son Henry Parsons land at Ammagansit... gives son Jeremiah Parsons land adjoining Josiah Mulford, and at Sandy Hood where he now lives... gives son Robbert lands after wife's term is out... gives two sons Jeremiah Parsons and Robbert Parsons remainder equally... executors: Jeremiah and Robbert Parsons ... witnesses: Ludlam Parsons, John, Mulford, John Straton. Proved 26 Sept. 1793 by Ludlam Parsons "weaver," and John Stratton "schoolmaster," both of Easthampton. Administration granted 26 Sept. 1793 to Jeremiah and Robert Parsons.

A-300. JOHN PARSONS, of Easthampton, 6 Oct. 1792... provides for wife Abigail... gives son John Parsons land bought of Samuel Conkling, Aaron Fithian, Lineus Conkling, David Fithian... gives son Stephen Parsons land adjoining that of Jeremiah Terry, deceased, and Ebenezer Hedges, Isaac Van Scoy, Daniel Hedges, also heirs of Benjamin Stratton, deceased, also land in Montauk, and land bought of Daniel Dayton, John Miller at Three Mile Harbor... gives daughter Elisabeth Ranger land adjoining that of her husband Samuel Ranger and Dominy... gives five grandsons, (sons of son Seth, deceased) Chatfield, Hedges, Seth, Andrew and Jehiel land adjoining that of James Fields, David Miller, land bought of Jeremiah Conkling and adjoining that of Lefffert Lefferts, John Gardiner, Daniel King, land bought of Eliazor Conkling, and land son Seth bought of Mulford Conkling... gives daughter-in-law Joanna, widow of son Seth, improvements on last item... gives granddaughter Abigail, daughter of son Seth, 50 pounds... gives daughter Puah Davis 50 pounds... gives grandson Thomas Tillinghart 10 pounds... gives grandson John Tillinghart 10 pounds... gives granddaughter Puah Tillingart 10 pounds... gives two granddaughters, (daughters of son-in-law Daniel Conkling) Mary

45

and Abigail five pounds each... gives son Elnathan Parsons land bought of William Hedges... executors: wife Abigail, son Elnathan and friend Abraham Miller... witnesses: Jonathan Tuthill, Robert Parsons Jr. Jonathan Stratton Conkling. Proved 26 Sept. 1793 by Jonathan Tuthill, Robert Parsons "cordwainer," and Jonathan Stratton Conkling "carpenter," all of Easthampton. Administration granted 26 Sept. 1793 to Elnathan Parsons.

A-303. HENRY DAYTON, of Easthampton, 3 July 1784... provides for wife Hannah with negress Dinah, 10 pounds and etc... gives daughter Deborah Conkling land at Stony Hill bought of Henry Conkling's executors... gives grandson DaytonTallmage 10 pounds... gives son Samuel Dayton, goods, stocks, money and negro Peter... executors: son Samuel Dayton and son-in-law Edward Conkling... witnesses: Joseph Robbins, Jeremiah Gardiner, Samuel Gardiner. Proved 26 Sept. 1793 by Jeremiah Gardiner. Administration granted 26 Sept. 1793 to Samuel Dayton.

A-305. ELIAS COOK, of Southampton, 1 Nov. 1792... gives son Stephen Cook land adjoining that of David Corwethy, John Hildreth, Phillip Howell, land in Quague and a negro Charles... gives grandson Jared Hair 20 pounds... gives grandson Henry Cook land bought by son Elias of David Howell... gives daughter Keturah Corwithey and her three daughters Mary, Parmele and Ann personals... instructs son Stephen to maintain grandson William Cook... gives three grandsons Silvanus, Nathan and Jared land... executors: Stephon and Henry Cook... witnesses: John Cook, Samuel Howell Jr.,Silvanus Howell Jr. Proved 26 Sept. 1793 by Samuel Howell Jr. Administration granted 26 Sept. 1793 to Stephen and Henry Cook.

A-308. NATHANIEL ROGERS, of Southampton, 7 Sept. 1792... gives wife Mary five pounds and use of windmill... gives daughter Abigail Sandford five shillings ... gives daughter Mehetabel Cook 20 shillings... gives daughter-in-law Martha Stuart 20 shillings... gives two sons Abraham and Sceva Rogers land equally divided... if Abraham have no children his share to go to Sceva and his heirs... executors: friend Caleb Rogers and wife Mary Rogers... witnesses: Matthew Foster, Hannah Goldsmith,

Joseph Goldsmith. Proved 27 Sept. 1793 by Matthew Foster and Hannah Goldsmith "spinster." Administration granted 2 Oct. 1793 to Caleb Rogers.

A-310. DAVID DOWNS, of Southold, 23 Aug. 1790... gives son David Downs land ... provides for wife Elizabeth Downs... gives daughter Mehetabel Cook 30 pound ... gives daughter Easter Petty 30 pounds... gives daughter Elisabeth Downs 50 pounds and home while single... executors: son David Downs and wife Elizabeth Downs... witnesses: David Conkling, Daniel Wells, Jeremiah Youngs. Proved 2 Oct. 1793 by David Conkling "physician." Administration granted 2 Oct. 1793 to David Downs and Elizabeth Downs.

A-312. DANIEL WELLS, of Riverhead,, 21 July 1793... gives eldest son Daniel Wells land in Broad Meadow... gives two grandchildren Isaiah Wells and Elijah Wells land bought of Richard Sweasy, adjoining that of William Benjamin, Elias Parshall, and land in Quague... gives grandson Daniel Wells land... gives son Daniel Wells use of grandsons' inheritance until Isaiah Wells is 21 and Elijah is 18... gives wife Joanna Wells provisions... gives daughter Temperance Tuthill 50 pounds... gives daughter Anna Fanning use of land bought of Jacob and John Wicks which is given at her death to grandson Daniel Wells Fanning... gives daughter Joanna Reeve land... gives daughter Patience Terry 50 pounds... gives dauhter Mary Tuthill land lately bought of Jeremiah Wells... gives mother-in-law Anna Youngs 60 pounds... executors: son Daniel Wells, two sons-in-law James Tuthill and Isaac T. Reeve... witnesses: Benjamin L'Hommedieu, David Wells, Nathaniel Wells Jr. Proved 2 Oct. 1793 by Benjamin L'Hommedieu "blacksmith," and David Wells. Administration granted 2 Oct. 1793 to Daniel Wells, James Tuthill and Isaac T. Reeve.

A-315. HENRY TUTHILL, of Southold, 13 Jan. 1793... gives wife Phebe estate... gives granddaughter Mary Short 20 pounds... gives granddaughter Anna Symmes 80 pounds... gives granddaughter Mary Wells 10 pounds... gives granddaughter Agurty (Agatha) Overton 10 pounds... gives granddaughter Phebe Goldsmith, when 18, silver spoons which "caust Eighteen

Shiling a peas"... gives grandson Tuthill Reeves personals... gives granddaughter Anny Symmes 10 pounds worth of goods... gives grandson Tuthill Reeves estate after wife, he to pay legacies... executors: wife Phebe and grandson Tuthill Reeve... witnesses: John Williamson, Mary Corwin,Mary Corwin Jr. Proved 2 Oct. 1793 by John Williamson. Administration granted 2 Oct. 1793 to Isaac Tuthill Reeve.

A-316. THOMAS CONKLING Sr., of Huntington, 11 Jan. 1793... to son Ezekiel Conkling half of land... gives nine children of son David Conkling, deceased, half of land to share alike except for grandson Thomas Conkling who gets half a share... gives son Hubboard Conkling 10 pounds... executors: son Ezekiel Conkling and friend John Ketcham ... witnesses: Philip Conkling, Solomon Ketcham, Amos Platt. Proved 21 Oct. 1793 by Solomon Ketcham. Administration granted 21 Oct. 1793 to Ezekiel Conkling and John Ketcham.

cA-318. NATHAN VALENTINE, of Huntington, 10 June 1790... gives two sons Nathan and Richard Valentine personals... instructs four children Richard and Nathan Valentine, Mary Stratton and Jean Carman to support the negroes... gives grandson Scudder Valentine lands at West Hills... gives grandson Gilbert Valentine, son of Nathan Valentine, land remaining... provides for wife Esther Valentine... gives son Richard 50 pounds... gives two daughters Mary Stratton and Jean Carman money remaining... executors; son Richard Valentine, son-in-law John Carman... witnesses: Foster Nostran, Charity Nostrand, Wilmot Oakley. Proved 8 Nov. 1793 by Wilmot Oakley of Queens County. Administration granted 8 Nov. 1793 to Richard Valentine and John Carman.

A-320. JOSEPH IRELAND, of Huntington, 31 Dec. 1784... executors to sell estate to best advantage of wife and children... gives wife Elizabeth Ireland eleventh part of estate... gives deceased son John Ireland's children a tenth of remainder equally divided between sons and daughters... gives daughter Sarah Jervis' children a tenth... gives daughter Phebe Oakley's children a tenth... gives son Daniel Ireland a tenth... gives daughter Margaret Jervis and her four children by Joshua Brush a tenth... gives son Joseph Ireland Jr. a tenth... gives daughter Elizabeth Smith a tenth... gives son Jacob Ireland a tenth... gives son Thomas Ireland a tenth... gives grandson Losee Ireland a tenth... executors: Samuel Wood and sons Jacob and Joseph Ireland, of Huntington... witnesses: John Oakley, Nathaniel Whitman, Harmon Lefford. Proved 8 Nov. 1793 by John Oakley and Nathaniel Whitman. Administration granted 8 Nov. 1793 to Samuel Wood, Jacob and Joseph Ireland.

A-323. JOSEPH CLEVELAND, of Southold, 13 Oct. 1793... provides for wife Marey... gives two daughters Abigail and Anna a home while single... gives son Joseph and son Lazarus all land equally, they to pay their brother Benjamin 55 pounds... mentions land formerly of Nathan Hains... gives daughters Mary and Mehetable an additional five pounds each... executors: sons Joseph, Lazarus and Benjamin... witnesses: Benjamin Horton, Joshua Reve, Jonathan Horton, son of Lazarus Horton, deceased. Proved 28 Nov. 1793 by Joshua Reeve and Jonathan Horton. Administration granted 28 Nov. 1793 to Joseph, Lazarus and Benjamin Cleveland.

A-325. JOSHUA LONGBOTTOM, of Brookhaven, cordwainer, 13 Sept. 1779... gives daughter Mary Longbottom land adjoining that of Allickseander Hawkins... gives daughter Ruth Roe land... gives daughter Julianah Longbottow land... gives daughter Sarah Longbottom land adjoining that of Isaac Davis, and 50 pounds.... gives grandson Joshua Dickinson, when of age, land adjoining that of Israel Hawkings and George Muirson... gives son Jonathan Dickinson moveables... executors: son John Roe, son Jonathan Dickinson and daughter Mary Longbottom... witnesses: Austin Roe, Abraham Cooper Woodhull, Nathan Woodhull Jr. Proved 1 Apr. 1794 by Austin Roeo "joiner." Administration granted I Apr. 1794 to Mary Muirson (one of the executors).

A-328. BENJAMIN SAYRE, of Southampton, blacksmith, 14 Nov. 1791... gives son David Sayre land formerly bought by father of Thomas Howell... gives son Benjainin Sayre land bought of William Topping, John Reeve, Silas Howell, and land adjoining that of Josiah Hands, Daniel Hedges, and land at

Easthampton adjoining that of Ezekiel Howell and Noah Barns... gives son James Sayre land bought of Joshua Howell... gives son David Sayre and son James Sayre equally land at Noyack and land adjoining that of John Norris, land bought of Abraham Cook,and adjoining land of Stephan Edward and Moses Howell... gives sons David, Benjamin and James Sayre land equally at Crooked Pond... gives son Zephaniah Sayre moveables... gives four daughters Susannah, Elizabeth, Phebe and Abigail five shillings each... executors: two sons David and James Sayre... witnesses: Josiah Cooper, Hannah Cooper, Elias Matthews. Proved 3 Apr. 1794 by Josiah Cooper "cordwainer." Administration granted 3 Apr. 1794 to David and James Sayre.

A-330. OBADIAH HOWELL, of Southampton, 2 July 1791... provides for wife Elizabeth... moveable estate to be sold... gives son Obadiah land formerly adjoining that of Capt. Obadiah Rogers, land at Shinecock... gives daughter Elizabeth 30 pounds and home while single... gives two sons Daniel and Henry remaining land equally divided... executors: brother Richard Howell, Henry White and Stephen Bishop... witnesses: William Halliock, Stephen Rayner, Silvanus Jagger. Proved 4 Apr. 1794 by William Halliock "marinrer." Administration granted 3 Apr.1794 to Henry White.

A-332. RICHARD HOWELL, of Southampton, 8 Oct. 1793... gives heirs of brother Obadiah Howell, deceased, all land and moveables... gives brother James Howell three pounds of a note against him.... gives brother Ryall Howell four pounds out of brother's note... gives brother Sylvanus Howell three pounds out of note... gives sister Abigail Stephens two pounds out of note... executors: brother Silvanus Howell, Henry White and William Herrick... witnesses: William R. Halloick, Joel Rayner, James Foster. Proved 4 Apr. 1794 by William E. Halloick "mariner." Administration granted 4 Apr. 1794 to Henry White.

A-334. JOHN WOODHULL, of Brookhaven, 13 Feb. 1790... gives son William Woodhull one pound...gives son John Woodhull one pound... gives son Caleb Woodhull land adjoining James Davis... gives son Merrett Smith Woodhull land adjoining that of John Miller, Thomas Helmes, fomerly Ebenezer Miller, and Isaac Miller... gives sons James, Gilbert and Jeffery Amherst Woodhull, equally, land adjoining that of Noah Hallock, land bought of Coll. Henry Smith... gives daughter Elizabeth Woodhull 15 pounds... gives sons Caleb and Merret Smith Woodhull remainder...executors: sons Caleb, Merret S., James and Gilbert Woodhull... witnesses: Nathaniel Davis, Caleb Helme, Daniel Hawkins. Proved 29 Apr. 1794 by Nathaniel Davis and Caleb Helme. Administration granted 29 Apr. 1794 to Merret Smith Woodhull.

cA-337. CALEB WOODHULL, of Brookhaven, farmer, 13 Aar. 1791... gives brother Merrett S. Woodhull land, provided he pay his brother Jeffery A. Woodhull 40 pounds... gives brother William Woodhull and Jeffery A. Woodhull and sister Elizabeth Hopkins 40 pounds each... executors: brother Merritt S. Woodhull and Nathaniel Davis second... witnesses: David Woodhall, Elizabeth Miller, Daniel Hawkins. Proved 29 Apr. 1794 by David Woodhull "physician."

A-339. OBADIAH SMITH,of Smithtown, 25 Apr. 1794... gives wife Anna negro Mingo, negress Zipporah and 15 pounds annually... gives two daughters Mary Woodhull and Ruth Carll, equally, negress Sarah, negro Francis, and a farm... gives son Addam negro Joseph, negresses Jane and Jude, and land... executor: son Addam and son-in-law Abraham Woodhull, son-in-law Timothy Carll and brother-in-law Epenetus Smith... witnesees: William Blydenburgh, Epenetus Smith, Richard Blydenburgh. Proved 12 May 1794 by William Blydenburgh "shopkeeper." Administration granted 12 May 1794 to Addam Smith and Abraham Woodhull.

A-341. ANANIAS BRUSH, of Huntington, 27 Feb. 1794... gives wife Judith a year's provisions and 120 pounds... gives her daughter Rebecka a calf... estate to be sold...gives Stephen Brush, son of son Nathaniel Brush, deceased, 100 pounds for his support... remainder divided equally between three children Zophar Brush, Susannah Ketcham and Phebe Conkling... executors: son Zophar Brush and friend Hennery Townsend... witnesses: Jacamiah Brush, Morris Barto, John Brush. Proved 16 May 1794 by Jacamiah Brush. Administration granted 16 May 1794 to Zophar Brush and Hennery Townsend.

51

A-344. LEMUEL BRYAN, of Huntington, 7 Apr. 1794...gives wife Elizabeth provisions and negro Charles... gives son Ebenezer land at Cow Harbor, Crab Meadow, and adjoining land of Jesse Bryan... gives son Alexander land adjoining that of Joel Rogers, Eliphalet Bunce, Malancton Bryan, land bought of Capt. Epenetus Smith... gives son Smith homestead adjoining land of John Vail... gives daughter Jemima 40 pounds... remainder divided equally between three daughters Trulove, Elisabeth and Jemima... three sons to be put to trades, and lands to rent until sons are of age... executors: Henry Scudder, Augustin Fleet and son-in-law Robert Rogers... witnesses: Joshua Hartt, Samuel Bunce, Robert Rogers. Proved 2 June 1794 by Joshua Hartt. Administration granted 2 June 1794 to Henry Scudder and Robert Rogers.

A-347. BENJAMIN GILDERSLEEVE, of Huntington, 27 Mar. 1792... provides for wife Elizabeth Gildersleeve... gives son Fitch Gildersleeve five shillings... gives two sons Jonas and Thomas Gildersleeve land equally, they to pay sons John and Phillip 10 pounds each... executors: son Jonas Gildersleeve, Zebulon Buffets ... witnesses: Pene Blackly, Phebe Rogers, Moses Blackly. Proved 2 June 1794 by Pene Blackly. Administration granted 2 June 1794 to Jonas Gildersleeve and Zebulon Buffets.

A-349. OBADIAH SMITH, of Smithtown, 7 June 1792... gives wife Sarah 300 pounds, and negress Bette... gives eldest son William land bought of John Gardiner, for life and then to grandson Siah (Isaiah)... gives son David land bought of Samuel Ketcham, land at Whitman's Hollow, Sunk Meadow Harbor... gives son Lucies land and negro Harry... gives two grandsons Thomas and Prior land, they to pay their sister Mary 100 pounds when she is 18... mentions all are under age... gives daughter-in-law Susannah to bring up children... residue to be sold an divided between three sons William, David and Lucies, and the three children of son Samuel, deceased... executors: sons David and Lucies Smith and Alexander Smith... witnesses: Pheletus Smith, Elias Smith, Ebenezer Alben. Proved 9 July 1794 by Philetus Smith. Administration granted 9 July 1794 to David, Lucies and Alexander Smith.

A-352. DAVID SANDFORD, of Southampton, 7 Feb. 1794...
gives son David Sandford land in Canoe Place... gives son
Lewis Sandford land... gives daughter Jane Sandford 60 pounds
and home while single ...gives daughter Anna Cook four
pounds... gives daughter Prudence Halsey eight pounds... gives
son Ezekiel Sandford remembrances ... gives son Matthew
Sandford six pounds...executor: son Lewis Sandford...
witnesses: Elisha Hallsey, Jason Loper, Elias Matthews. Proved
9 Sept.1794 by Elisha Hallsey. Administration granted 9 Sept.
1794 to Lewis Sandford.

A-354. JEREMIAH MILLER of Easthampton, 12 Feb. 1794...
provides for wife Ruth Miller... gives son Jeremiah Miller land
bought of Daniel Baker's heirs, Lemuel Hedges, Daniel Leek,
land at Occabonnock and Montaukit, land adjoining that of
Elisha Mulford, Daniel Hedges, Abraham Gardinir... gives son
Huntting Miller land adjoining that of Aaron Isaacs Jr., "my son
Huntting Mulford," David Stratton, Abraham Barns, land bought
of Elias Hedges, Burnet Miller, and land at Napeag ...gives
daughter Mary Buell 200 pounds... gives grandson Silvanuse
Miller 20 pounds and to be in care of wife... exocutors: wife Ruth,
sons Jeremiah and Huntting Miller... witnesses: John Chatfield,
Jeremiah Conkling, Henry Chatfield. Proved 9 Sept. 1794 by
John and Henry Chatfield. Administration granted 9 Sept.1794
to Jeremiah and Huntting Miller.

A-357. JONAS DAVIS, of Brookhaven, 20 Mar. 1794... gives
wife Tabitha Davis provisions which, at her death, descend to
daughters Elizabeth Davis, Tabitha Mills, Sybil Davis and Charity
Davis... gives son Jonas Davis land adjoining that of Jonathan
Hallock... gives daughter Elizabeth Davis 30 pounds and home
while single... gives daughter Tabitha Mills 30 pounds... gives
daughter Sybil Davis 30 pounds... gives daughter Charity Davis
30 pounds... executors: wife Tabitha Davis and son-in-law
George Mills... witnesses: Caleb Davis, John Smith, John Curtis.
Proved 19 Sept. 1794 by Caleb Davis. Administration granted 19
Sept. 1794 to Tabitha Davis and George Mills.

A-360. MARY MILLS, of Smithtown, 25 May 1787... gives sister
Martha Rowe linen... gives son Israel 12 pounds... gives son

Jacob remainder, but if he not marry his share reverts to son Israel and his heirs... executors: friends brother Phillips Rowe, Jonas Hawkins... witnesses: William Mills, Samuel Mills. Proved 14 Nov. 1794 by William Mills. Administration granted 14 Nov. 1794, to Phillips Rowe and Jonas Hawkins.

A-362. WILLIAM HALLOCK, of Riverhead, 19 June 1794... estate to be sold... gives eldest son William 200 pounds... gives two other sons Benjamin and Samuel 50 pounds each at 21 and a trade...gives two eldest daughters Hannah and Patience five pounds each... gives two youngest daughters Lydia and Mary 20 pounds each at 18... remainder equally divided between children William, Hannah, Patience, Benjamin, Lydia, Samuel and Mary... executors: son William and friend Ezra Corwin... witnesses: David Conkling, Jonathan Howell, Abraham King. Proved 26 Nov.1794 by Abraham King. Administration granted 26 Nov. 1794 to William Hallock and Ezra Corwin.

A-365. DAVID WOODRUFF, of Southampton, "being sick, 15 Nov. 1794... provides for wife Elizabeth... gives daughter Prudence Topping bedding... gives daughter Mary Terry five shillings... gives son Joshua Woodruff book... gives granddaughter Temperance Woodruff 25 pounds when of age... gives granddaughter Harriet Woodruff 25 pounds when of age... gives two grandsons Sylvester and Hallsey Woodruff 60 pounds when 21... gives grandson James Woodruff land, negro son of negress Rachel, a negro Cyrus for six months, he then to be freed... executors: friends David Hains and Jesse Woodruff... witnesses: Silas Woodruff, Elias Woodruff, Silas Woodruff Jr. Proved 23 Jan. 1795 by Silas, Elias and Silas Woodruff Jr. Administration granted 23 Jan. 1795 to David Hains and Jesse Woodruff.

A-367. WILLIAM TAYLOR, of Smithtown, "in weak and low state," 2 Mar. 1795... provides for wife Tabitha...provides for "expences of fixing Polly Totten agreeable to her indenture"... gives daughter Hannah remainder of personal estate... gives two sons Jonas and Mordecai money from sale of land equally divided... executors: friends John Vail and Isaac Buffet... witnesses: Simeon Totten, Edmund Totten, John Stratton.

Proved 24 Mar. 1795 by Simeon and Edmund Totten "coopers." Administration granted 24 Mar. 1795 to John Vail and Isaac Buffet.

A-369. JOSIAH WICKS, of Huntington, 31 Mar. 1783... gives son Seth Wickes land, with reversion to his brother Joshua Wickes... gives son Joshua 50 pounds when 21... gives son Solomon land bought from Moses Wickes... gives son Joshua 50 pounds when 24... gives daughters moveables, the lame daughter to half share more than the rest... provides for wife and maintenance of children... executors: Silas Carll of Huntington, Paul Theadore Smith and Caleb Smith Jr. of Smithtown... witnesses: Peter Garson, Ambrose Wickes, Martha Smith. Executors and Widow Sarah Wickes relinquished the executorship in writing 26 Mar. 1784. Proved 24 Mar.1795 by Lemuel Wickes and Moses Wickes swearing to testators signature, Ambrose Wickes and Martha Smith having died and Peter Garson not in the state as far as they know... Moses Wickes believes it was Garson's signature, and Lemuel Wickes recognizes his brother Ambrose Wickes' handwriting. Administration granted 24 Mar. 1795 to Seth Wickes "mariner" of Smithtown.

A-372. ZACCHEUS GOLDSMITH, (prob. of Islip) 3 Oct. 1794... gives grandson Daniel Goldsmith estate... gives son Daniel Goldsmith maintenance for life... gives daughter Mary Wickham's children and great-granddaughter Hellen Hudson 35 pounds equally divided... executors: grandson Daniel Goldsmith and friend James W. Booth... witnesses: Joshua Salmon, Joshua Hobart Booth, William Terry. Proved I Apr. 1795 by Joshua Salmon. Administration granted I Apr. 1795 to Daniel Goldsmith and James W. Booth.

A-374. JONATHAN SMITH, of Brookhaven, 18 Mar. 1786... provides for wife Catharine Smith... gives son Zephaniah Smith land adjoining that of Benjamin Smith, formerly Robert Akerly, deceased... in default of heirs, to Jonathan Smith Cetcham (Ketcham), daughter Phebe's eldest son... gives four daughters Temperance, Phebe, Catharine and Eunice land and money... gives daughters Catharine and Eunice home while single... executors: son Zephaniah Smith, Charles Jeffery Brewster and

Timothy Smith... witnesses: Timothy Smith, Ruth Smith, James Smith. Proved 7 Apr.1795 by James Smith. Administration granted 7 Apr. 1793 to Zephaniah Smith and Charles Jeffery Brewster.

A-375. JESSE SMITH, of Corum in Brookhaven, 22 Nov. 1794... gives son James Smith and bought of Richard Hudson and William Sell... reminder to be sold and proceeds to be for bringing up of children... gives eldest daughter Sarah Smith two pounds... gives daughter Rachel Smith two pounds... gives two sons Jonathan and Peter Smith money remaining equally divided... executors: wife Rachel Smith and Caleb M. Hulse... witnesses: Caleb M. Hulse, James Smith, Benjamin Overton. Proved 7 Apr. 1795 by James Smith third, of Corum. Administration granted 7 Apr. 1795 to Rachel Smith and Caleb M. Hulse.

A-377. JAMES TUTHILL, of Southold, 14 Nov. 1791... gives eldest son James Tuthill rights in Cutchogue Manor... gives second son David Tuthill land which was father Joshua Tuthill's... gives third son John Tuthill five pounds... gives fourth son Joshua Tuthill land, he to pay John Tuthill 50 pounds... gives five eldest daughters Elisabeth Howell, Abigail Downs, Hannah Swasey, Mehetabel Davies, and Lida Conkling five shillings each... gives youngest daughter Harmony Tuthill as much as to make her equal with her sisters at 18 or marriage... provides for wife Elizabeth Tuthill... executors: two sons James and David Tuthill... witnesses: Joseph H. Goldsmith, Abigail Goldsmith, Sarah Fleet. Proved 16 Apr. 1795 by Sarah Fleet "spinster." Administration granted 16 Apr. 1795 to James and David Tuthill.

A-379. JOHN TUTHILL, of Southold, farmer, 3 Feb. 1793 ... gives son John Tuthill whole estate ... provides wife with dower rights ... gives daughter Lydia Youngs 20 pounds and 40 shillings a year from son John ... executors: friends Daniel and Joseph Terry ... witnesses: Thomas Vail Jr., Nathaniel KingJr. Administration granted 17 Apr. 1795 to John Tuthill, deceased, when executors relinquished executorship.

A-382. JOSEPH BOOTH, of Southold, 7 Feb. 1794 ... executors to sell land bought of Orange Webb, and at Oyster Ponds, also passage boat called "Sterling Packet" ... provides for wife Elizabeth until son William Actin is 21 ... gives son Constant and son William reminder of land if they pay three sons Victor,Joseph and Henry 50 pounds each when 21, and daughters Fanny and Catie (Kate) Maria each 40 pounds when 18 ... gives daughter Elisabeth Webb 40 pounds ... provides life maintenance for negress Doll ... executors to free negro Reuben on 1 Jan. 1797 ... executors: wife Elizabeth, son Constant Booth, and friend Calvin Moore ... witnesses: David Fanning. Administration granted 30 June 1795 to Elizabeth Booth and Calvin Moore.

A-384. EPHRAIM L'HOMMEDIEU, of Easthampton, 3 Apr. 1796 ... executors to sell land bought of John Hand, Obadiah Gildersleeve ... provides for wife Mehitable with 50 pounds ... gives daughter Nancy 130 pounds when of age ... gives son Jabez Foster remainder of estate. Proved 1 July 1795 bv Samuel L'Hommadieu. Administration granted 1 July 1795 to Samuel L'Hommedieu.

A-386. CHARLES WHITE, of Southampton, farmer, 28 July 1791 ... executors to sell land adjoining that of Silas Cooper ... gives son-in-law Lemuel Hallsey land ... gives grandson Jesse Hallsey land ... provides for wife Sarah White ... mentions three sons-in-law Jesse Hallsey, Lemuel Hallsey and Samuel L'Hommedieu ... gives three daughters Charity Hallsey, Abigail Hallsey and Sarah L'Hommediou remainder of land ... executors: wife Sarah White, sons-in-law Jesse Hallsey, Lemuel Hallsey, Samuel L'Hommedieu ... witnesses: Joseph Gibbs, Daniel Gibbs, Jonathan Squier. Proved 1 July 1795 by Jonathan Squier. Administration granted 1 July 1795 to Lemuel Hallsey.

A-338. JACOB DOW, of Huntington, 21 3eb. 1795 ... gives daughter Hannah a bed ... provides for wife Phebe ... gives sons Phillip and Samuel 10 shillings each ... gives son Joseph land ... gives sons Joseph and Thomas timber land equally ... if Thomas neither marries of comes of age his share reverts to Joseph ... executors: son Joseph Dow and Garrett Montfort ... witnesses:

Jacob Seaman, Garret Montfoort, Amos Higbie. Proved 7 Aug. 1795 by Garret Monfoort "miller," and Amos Higbie. Administration granted 7 Aug. 1795 to Joseph Dow.

A-390. MICAH PHILLIPS, of Brookhaven, mariner, verbally, 19 Aug. 1795, on deathbed ... gives sister Deborah Phillips three-quarters of estate ... quarter of estate to be held in trust by uncle Jonas Phillips to be apportioned out at discretion to brother George Phillips ... recorded 26 Aug. 1795 ... the testator died on 21 Aug. 1795 ... witnesses: Jonas Hawkins, Katharine Hawkins, Deborah Hawkins. Proved 12 Sept. 1795 bv Jonas Hawkins, Ruth Hawkins and Deborah Hawkins. Administration granted 12 Sept. 1795 to Deborah Phillips of Smithtown.

A-392. DANIEL SMITH, of Smithtown, 2 Mar. 1792 ... provides for wife ... gives brother Micah land in Stonybrook Harbor and Long Beach ... gives brother Micah's son land in Smithtown ... gives William Rudyard, son of Thomas Rudyard, land where his father lives ... gives brother Obadiah a cane ... executors: wife and Philetus Smith ... witnesses John Wright, John Floyd, Woodhull Smith. Proved 19 Sept. 1795 by John Floyd. Administration granted 19 Sept. 1795 to Tabitha Smith and Philetus Smith.

A-394. SILVANUS PIERSON, of Sagg in Southampton, 21 Aug. 1795 ... gives daughter Rebekah two pounds ... gives daughter Martha seven pounds ... gives daughter Sarah four Pounds ... gives daughter Margaret 20 shillings ... gives three daughters; Martha, Sarah and Margaret three-quarters of estate equally divided ... the other quarter of estate to executors ... executors brother Timothy Pierson and friends David Hedges and Samuel Hainse Rose ... witnesses: Ebenezer White, Ezekiel Howell, Hugh Malcom. Proved 7 Nov. 1795 by Ezekiel Howell, "farmer." Administration granted 7 Nov. 1795 to Timothy Pierson and Samuel Hains Rose.

A-396. SAMUEL HAINS of Southhampton, farmer, 24 Aug. 1794 ... provides for wife Sarah Hain ... gives Phebe Howell, wife's daughter, two gowns that were former wife's ... gives Hannah Howell two pounds ... gives only son Job Hains land with reversion to brother David Hains, nephew Stephen Hains, and two brothers James and Daniel Hains ... executor brother David Rains ... witnesses: Abegail Sandford, Caleb Corwithe, Stephen Hains. Proved 7 Nov. 1795 by Stephen Hains. Administration granted 7 Nov. 1795 to David Hains.

A-399. JOHN HILDRETH, of Southampton, 'very sick," 30 Dec. 1794 ... provides for wife Mehetabel ... gives son Isaac Hildreth land once father's, land bought of James Hildreth, of trustees of Southampton, land adjoining that of John Cook, William Halsey, Samuel Howell, John Gelston, Josiah Cooper, Paul Halsey, Stephen Hallsey ... gives son Septimus Hildreth land adjoining David Corwithe, Stephen Cook ... gives son Luther land ... gives son John Hildreth land ... gives daughter Elisabeth Rogers five pounds ... gives daughter Sarah Halsey 40 shillings ... gives daughter Anna Bebee 20 shillings ... gives daughter Polly 50 pounds to be in trust to Dr. Henry White of Southampton until she is 18 ... Septimus Hildreth is sick; if he dies his property goes to other three sons ... executors: sons Isaac and Septimus Hildreth and friend Samuel Howell, all of Southampton ... witnesses Elias Matthews, Matthew E. Cooper, Uriah Miller. Proved 7 Nov. 1795 by Matthew H. Cooper. Administration granted 7 Nov. 1795 to Isaac Hildreth and Samuel Howell.

A-402. JOHN GARDINER, of Southold, 17 May 1793 ... gives son John Gardiner apparel ... relieves son James of all debts ... estate to be sold and divided between four grandchildren Jeter (sic) Gardiner, Fletcher Gardiner, Eunice Gardiner and Elizabeth Gardiner ... gives son John Gardiner a fifth share ... gives son Jared Gardiner a fifth ... gives son Benjamin Gardiner a fifth ... gives daughter Gardiner a fifth ... frees negro Cuff, all other negroes over 30 set free and remainder when 30 ... executors: William Horton and sons John and Benjamin Gardiner, and friend Daniel Osborn ... witnesses: Daniel Osborn, Mary Osborn, Anna Clark. Proved 7 Nov. 1795 by Daniel Osborn "att. at Law." Administration granted 7 Nov. 1795 to William Horton and John and Benjamin Gardiner.

A-406. JOHN BRUSH, of Huntington, 29 Oct. 1795 ... gives son John mills and land ... gives son Jesse 500 pounds ... gives daughters Truelove and Fanny 180 pounds in cash and 80 pounds worth of moveables each ... gives son John negro Absalom until 1 Apr. 1797 and then free him ... gives four sons Ebenezer, Ichabod, Jesse and Samuel Scudder two-thirds of remainder ... gives three daughters Rebecca, Freelove and Fanny one-third ... orders son John to pay son Samuel Scudder 400 pounds in two years ... executors: son John, and Thomas Rowe ... witnesses: Ebenezer Platt, James Roe, Ebenezer B. Brush ... Proved 18 Nov. 1795 by Ebenezer Platt. Administration granted 18 Nov. 1795 to John Brush and Thomas Rowe.

A-408. DR. JAMES SANDFORD, of Huntington, 2 Oct. 1795 ... Gives wife Elizabeth provisions ... executors to sell estate for support and education of children ... executors: wife Elisabeth, Henry Scudder Lewis ... witnesses: Alexander Dunton, Benjamin Coddington, Mary Thompson. Proved 18 Nov. 1795 by Alexander Dunton and Mary Thompson. Administration granted 18 Nov. 1795 to Elisabeth Sandford.

A-410. JOSEPH JAYNE, of Smith town, 22 Apr. 1795 ... provides for wife Tabitba Jayne ... gives son Joseph Jayne 10 shillings ... gives daughter Catharine Dar ling 10 shillings ... gives daughter Ruth Darling 10 shillings ... gives daughter Tabitha Jones 25 pounds ... gives two daughters Hannah Tyler and. Bethsheba Jayne 50 pounds each ... gives son Peter Jayne land ... gives son Ebenezer Jayne remaining land and moveables ... executors: wife Tabitha Jayne, son Joseph Jayne and son-in-law Hamilton Darling ... witnesses: Isaac Smith, Morris Jayne, Stephen Jayne. Proved 18 Nov. 1795 by Isaac Smith. Administration granted 18 Nov.1795 to Tabitha Jayne, Joseph Jayne, Hamilton Darling.

A-413. JONATHAN JARVIS, of Huntington, 8 Apr. 1788..,.gives wife Charity Jarvis provisions ... gives son William Jarvis land ... gives son Timothy Jarvis land adjoining that of Joseph Lewis, deceased, David Rusco, Zebulon Platt, Zophar Platt, Israel Wood ... gives son Isaiah Jarvis a cow ... gives granddaughter Phebe Jarvis 20 pounds when 18 or married ... executors: friends John Wickes, Epenetus Conkling, and wife Charity Jarvis ... witnesses: Zophar Platt, Zabulon Platt, John Ketcham. Proved

17 Dec. 1795 by Zophar and Zebulon Platt. Administration granted 17 Dec. 1795 to John Wickes and Epenetus Conkling.

A-416. STEPHEN WHITE, of Huntington, 20 Nov. 1795 ... gives son Israel White land & and money ... Gives two daughters Sarah Carll and Martha Samms 30 pounds each ... executors: friend Samuel Oakley, son Israel White, both of Huntington ... witnesses Selah Wood, Nathaniel Whitman, Richard Oakley. Codicil 21 Nov.1795 to dispose of stock ... same witnesses. Proved 17 Dec. 1795 by Selah Wood. Administration granted 17 Dec. 1795 to Samuel Oakley and Israel White.

A-419. STEPHEN GERARD, of Brookhaven, being sick, 3 Sept. 1795 ... provides for wife Elizabeth Gerrard ... gives father Benjamin Gerrard estate for life ... gives brother Nathaniel Gerrard estate at father's death ... executors: wife Elisabeth and father Benjamin ... witnesses; John Curtis, Isaac Gerrard, Vary Gerrard. Proved 4 Jan. 1796 by John Curtis, Isaac Gerrard, Mary Gerrard. Administration granted 4 Jan. 1796 to Elizabeth Gerrard, Benjamin Gerrard.

A-420. BENJAMIN STRONG, of Islip, 22 Apr. 1793 ... executors to sell land adjoining that of Stephen Abbet ... reminder to be in hands of wife Elisabeth Strong and son Samuel Strong until youngest children are of full age ... then to sell all remaining estate and divide. ..gives four sons Samuel Thompson Strong, Benajah Strong, William Strong and Silas C. Strong three-quarters estate equally ... gives four daughters Mary Strong, Nancy Strong, Elizabeth Strong and Hannah Strong a quarter of estate equally ... -gives three oldest daughters first wife's furniture ... executors: brother-in-law Isaac Thompson, wife Elizabeth, son Samuel T. Strong ... witnesses: Anking Habra, Stephen Abbet, Joshua Hart. Proved 11 Feb. 1796 by Stephan Abbot. Administration granted 11 Feb. 1796 to Elizabeth Strong and Samuel T. Strong.

A-423. ROBERT TERRY, of Brookhaven, I June 1782 ... provides for wife Patience ... gives son John Terry land ... gives grandson Robert Woodhull land at son John's death ... gives grandson Nathaniel Woodhull 100 pounds ... gives daughters

61

Hannah and Patience 10 pounds ... executors Joseph Brown. Patience Terry, wife, and John Terry, son ... witnesses: David Brown, Daniel Brown, Isaac Brown. Proved 13 Feb. 1796 by Daniel Brown.

A-424. HENRY BISHOP, of Huntington, 17 May 1795 ... gives two nephews James and Harry Bishop (James being son of brother John, and Harry being son of brother Jonah) all land equally divided ... gives two sisters Abigail and Jemima moveables ... gives two brothers John and Jonah apparel ... executors: John and Jonah Bishop ... witnesses Samuel Bunch, Elisabeth Brasier (Bunce), Henry Scudder. Proved 2 Mar. 1796 by Samuel Bunce "carpenter." Administration granted 2 Mar. 1796 to John and Jonah Bishop.

A-426. ELEAZER HAWKINS, of Brookhaven, 20 Aug. 1795 ... gives wife Mary 25 pounds ... executors to sell land, cider mill "between me and my brother Benjamin Hawking,, ... gives son Elanathan a trade and money at 21 ... gives daughter Mary 100 pounds at 18 ... gives sister Martha Brewster 10 pounds ... gives sister Elisabeth Hawkins 25 pounds ... executors wife : Mary, Jacob Hawkins and Jediah Williamson.. witnesses: David Cleves, Nathaniel Tooker, Gilbert Hulse. Proved 7 Mar. 1796 by Gilbert Rules and Nathaniel Tooker. Administration granted 7 Mar. 1796 to Jacob Hawkins and Jediah Williamson.

A-428. REBEKAH SCUDDER, of Smithtown, 20 Sept. 1795 ..., gives granddaughter Sary Haff furniture ... gives all sisters of Sary Haff five shillings each ... gives granddaughter Rebakar Jarvis 20 shillings ...gives granddaughter Margit Diser bedding ... gives great-grandson John Jervis 20 shillings ... gives Sary Haff remainder of estate ... executors: Nathaniel Bigs and Van Haelah Robbins ... signed Rebecca Scudder ... witnesses: Smith Brush, Samuel Brush, Isaac Burr. Proved 28 Mar. 1796 by Samuel Brush. Administration granted 28 Mar. 1796 to Nathaniel Biggs and Van Haelah Robbins.

A-429. WILLIAM CASE, of Southold, being aged, 31 Dec. 1793 ... gives daughter Anne five shilling ... gives daughter Prudence and daughter Abigail five shillings each ... gives son James

Case land ... executor: son James Case ... witnesses: Samuel Davids, James W. Booth, Benjamin Hutchinson. Proved 30 Mar. 1796 by Samuel Davids and James W. Booth. Administration granted 30 Mar. 1796 to James Case.

A-430. PHEBE SANDFORD, of Southhampton, 28 Sept. 1790 ... gives daughter Phebe Sandford land at Calf Creek, and land adjoining that of William and Nathaniel Rogers ... gives son Nathan Sandford land at Easthampton ... executors: friends Jonathan Rogers and David Haine ... witnesses; Joseph Goodale, Daniel Stratton. Proved 30 Mar. 1796 by Joseph Goodall. Administration granted 30 Mar. 1796 to Jonathan Rogers and David Fains.

A-432. WILLIAM KINNER, of Brookhaven, 8 May 1795, very sick ... gives wife Mary estate ... gives son Jeremiah Kinner half of schooner for 20 pounds ... gives son Selah Kinner land adjoining that of Spuer Davis, Phillips Brown ... gives son Jonathan Kinner half of sloop ... remaining estate to be divided between four children William, Jeremiah, Selah and Phebe ... executors: Samuel Hopkins, Timothy Davis ... witnesses: Daniel Comstock, Nancy Rowe, Abigail Brown. Proved 5 Apr. 1796 by Daniel Constock, "phisician" Administration granted 5 Apr.1796 to Samuel Hopkins and Timothy Davis.

A-434. BENJAMIN NEWTON, of Smithtown, 10 Nov. 1787 ... provides for wife Mary Newton ... gives three daughters Sary L'Hommediou, Mary Hawkins and Elisabeth Hawkins stock and furniture ... remembers son John Newton ... gives grandson James Newton land, with reversion to three daughters and son ... executors: friends John Hawkins, John Newton, William Hawkins ... witnesses: William Blydonburgh, Joseph Hudson, William Tooker. Proved 5 Apr. 1796 by William Tooker. Administration granted 5 Apr. 1796 to John Newton.

A-435. STEPHEN JAGGER, of Southampton, 5 Dec. 1795 ... gives wife Mariam 30 pounds ... gives son David land in Riverhead ... gives son Jonathan land ... gives son Enoch land ... gives son George Whitfield 400 pounds and land lately bought of Capt. Halsey in Woodhull, Montgomery County Co., N.Y. ...

four daughters Susana, Hana, Abigail and Anne 50 pounds each ... executors: son Enoch and son-in-law William Halsey ... witnesses: Hugh Raynor, James Raynor, Esther Raynor. Proved 21 Apr. 1796 by Hugh and James Raynor. Administration granted 21 Apr.1796 to Enoch Jagger and William Halsey.

A-439. NOAH WETMORE (WHITMORE), of Brookhaven, 7 Mar. 1796 ... provides for wife Submit ... gives oldest son Noah 10 Pounds ... gives daughter Irene five pounds ... gives three sons Noah, Appolos and Samuel Ithiel, and daughter Irene the reversion of estate at their mother's death ... executors: wife Submit Wetmore (Whitmore) and Selah Strong ... witnesses: Abraham Woodhull, Samuel Thompson, Daniel Comstock. Will proved 26 Apr. 1796 by Abraham Woodhull and Daniel Comstock. Administration granted 26 Apr. 1796 to Submit Wetmore (Whitmore) and Selah Strong. [The surrogates wrote "Noah Whitmore's will" on this in 1796.]

A-441. MARY JONES, widow of Southampton, 16 Jan. 1796 ... gives granddaughter Mary Talmage five pounds ... gives granddaughter Catherine Clarkson five pounds ... gives grandson Nicoll Floyd five pounds ... gives daughter Phebe Howell, grandson Elias Jones and granddaughter Elizabeth Jones moveables equally divided ... witnesses: Samuel Comer, Henry Halsey, Elias Jones. Proved I May 1796 by Henry Halsey. Administration granted 1 May 1796 to Elias Jones of Southampton, grandson of deceased.

A-443. DAVID HOWELL, of Southampton, 26 May 1792 ... gives wife Phebe Howell 20 pounds ... gives son David Howell land at Montauk, land bought of Mayor Silas Cook ... gives grandson Charles Howell land adjoining that of Benjamin Fausters (Foster) ... gives son Abraham Howell land at Ketchabonack ... gives son Stephen Howell land and stock ... gives son Matthew Howell land at Flying Point, Canoe Place, Tianer, Cow Neck, and to pay son David Howell 150 pounds ... give grandson Silas Howell land adjoining that of Joseph Hildreth ... orders son Matthew to pay two daughters Damaris and Pamelia 50 pounds each ... gives grandson Malby Gelston 30 pounds ... executors: sons David, Stephen, Abraham and

Matthew ... witnesses: Elias Harris, Elisha Sandford, William Herrick. Proved 2 May 1796 by Elias Harris.

A-444. MARY SHAW, wife of Daniel Shaw, of Southold, 29 Aug. 1791 ... gives two sons Daniel and Josiah Shaw equally lands given "me by my father Josiah Youngs" ... gives daughter Hannah Shaw home while single with 30 pound dower when married ... executor: husband Daniel Shaw ... witnesses: David Williamson, Gamaliel King, Nathaniel Wells Jr. Proved 4 May. 1796 by David Williamson. (see below)

A-445. DANIEL SHAW, of Riverhead, 8 Sept. 1795 ... gives two sons Daniel and Josiah estate equally divided ... gives daughter Hannah 30 pounds mentioned in wife's will (the previous one) when married, 10 pounds extra and home while single or 20 pounds more ... executors: David Conkling and son Daniel (also to execute will of wife deceased) ... witnesses: Daniel Youngs. Prudence Tuthill, David Conkling. Proved 4 May 1796 by Daniel Youngs. Administration granted 4 May 1796 to David Conkling and Daniel Shaw.

A-447. WILLIAM DICKINSON, of Riverhead, being sick, 25 Apr.1796 ... executors to sell estate ... gives son David Dickerson 100 pounds ... gives son Abraham Dickerson 10 shillings ... .gives five daughters Abigail, Mary, Bethiah, Ruaner,.. Matthew (sic. perhaps Matty) five pounds each ... gives sons Jonathan Dickerson, William Dickerson, Benjamin Dickerson, John Dickerson, Elisah Dickerson, Elijah Dickerson reminder equally divided ... executors: sons Jonathan and William Dickerson ... witnesses: Obadiah Wells, Richard Brown, Christopher Brown. Proved 5 May 1796 by Obadiah Wells. Administration granted 5 May 1796 to Jonathan Dickerson. (The name is Dickinson.)

A-448. STEPHEN DAVIS, of Smithtown, 21 Apr 1796 ... gives wife Martha Davis 20 pounds ... gives oldest daughter Mary Davis and Abigail Davis land in Islip equally divided ... gives two youngest daughters Martha Davis and Caturah Davis land equally divided ... gives Caturah Davis 10 pounds ... Executors: friends John Newton, Caleb Newton ... witnesses: John Newton,

Abel Biggs, Deborah Biggs. Proved 14 May 1796 by Abel Biggs. Administration granted 14 May 1796 to John and Caleb Newton.

A-450. WILLIAM NICOLL, of Islip, 17 Dec, 1751 ... executors to pay legacies of will of father William Nicoll, deceased ... personal estate to be sold and put out to interest for upkeep and education of son Henry Nicoll until 21 ... but should Henry become heir entail of his grandfather, my estate goes to my wife ... son William is heir of his grandfather's estate and not of age ... executors: wife Francis, brother Benjamin Nicoll and friends William Cook of New York, John Grindle of New York "mariner," and Isaac Thompson ... witnesses: John Riker, James Arden, John Rapalye Jr., Samuel Clayton. Proved 24 June 1796 by James Arden "merchant" of New York. Administration granted 24 June 1796 to William Terry of Islip, a creditor of testator.

A-452. ISAIAH REEVE, of Brookhaven, 15 Oct. 1795 ... given son Silas Reeve estate for life and than to his two sons Charles and Joel Reeve equally divided ... gives daughter Abigail Post five shillings annually, and if she have an heir it gets 40 pounds ... gives daughter Elizabeth Homan 50 pounds ... gives daughter Juliana Reeve three pounds annually and home while single and 50 pounds when married ... gives daughter Mehitable Bushup, (Bishop) 30 pounds ...gives four granddaughters Abigail, Catherine, Elizabeth and Marah Homan 10 pounds each ... executors: son Silas Reeve and John Havens Jr ... witnesses: Zachariah Sandford, Mary Cooper, John Havens Jr. Proved 29 June 1796 by Zachariah Sandford. Administration granted 29 June 1796 to Silas Reeve and John Havens Jr.

A-455. JOB VALENTINE, of Huntington, 13 Mar. 1789. ..estate equally divided is, given to nephew Richard Valentine, niece Gean Carman wife of John Carman of Huntington, to sister Mary Vandewater, nephew John Vandewater son of sister Mary, to my niece Mary Lewis wife of James Lewis Jr. of South Hempstead in Queens County, and to Hester Johnson (a niece) wife of Dorian Johnson of Reddington in New Jersey, and to sister Amy Jackson ... executors: friend Richard Valentine of North Hempstead, Queens County, Richard Valentine and John Carman of Huntingdon, Suffolk County ... witnesses: William

Williams, Austin Williams, Richard Valentine, of Queens. Proved 12 Aug. 1796 by Richard Valentine of Queens. Administration granted 12 Aug 1796 to John Carman and Richard Valentine (probably of Queens).

A-456. EZEKIEL BRUSH, of Huntington, 27 July 1785 ... provides for wife Mary Brush ... gives son Jacamiah Brush estate at wife's death and land adjoining that of Daniel Nostron ... gives son Benjamin Brush land in Bating Place ... gives grandson James Brush land adjoining that of Eliphalet Chichester, Selah Woods, Malby Burtis (Curtis?) when 21 ... Jacamiah to have use of land, grandson James to be put out to trade ... gives Jacamiah and Benjamin Brush rights in Oyster Bay ... gives daughter Mary Smith and granddaughter Anne Smith (under age and single) proceeds from sale of moveables ... executors: son Jacamiah Brush, son-in-law Richard Smith and friend John Oakley ... witnesses: Zophar Brush, Richard Brush, David Peersall. Proved 16 Sept. 1796 by Richard Brush. Administration granted 16 Sept. 1796 to Jacamiah Brush.

A-458. DAVID YOUNGS, of Moriches in Brookhaven, 29 Aug. 1796 ... very sick ... provides for wife Catharine ... gives son David Youngs third of estate when 21 ... gives daughters Elisabeth Deiker (Decker?) and Bethiah Havens third of estate equally divided ... executors: wife Catharine Youngs and David Day ... witnesses: John Bishop, Gorg Corvert, David Day. Proved 20 Sept. 1796 by George Covet. Administration granted 20 Sept. 1796 to Catharine Youngs, David Day.

A-460. PHINEAS FANNING, (probably of Southold) 30 May 1796 ... gives two daughters Esther Hudson and Mehetable Jagger the whole estate ... negro Comus to have freedom ... executors: Henry Hudson and Enoch Jagger ... witnesses: Joseph Parker Wickham, Obadiah Hudson, Isaiah Benjamin. Proved 23 Sept. 1796 by Obadiah Hudson. Administration granted 23 Sept. 1796 to Henry Hudson and Enoch Jagger.

A-461. THOMAS WICKHAM, of Southold, 12 Sept. 1796 ... estate to brother Norris Wickham and his wife for life and then to Thomas Wickham, son of brother Norris Wickham ...

executors: brother Norris Wickham and nephew Thomas Wickham ... witnesses: Thome Webb, Jarred Landon, Calvin Wells. Proved 9 Nov. 1796 by Thomas Webb. Administration granted 9 Nov. 1796 to Norris Wickham.

A-462. ASA KING, of Southold, 4 Sept. 1796 ... provides for wife Mary King an Indian girl Jude indentured and provided for ... gives brother Samuel King personal estate remaining ... gives cousin Barnabas Tuthill six pounds and to my sister living five pounds ... executors: friends Nathaniel King, Daniel Tuthill, Christopher Brown ... witnesses: Sylvester Lester, David Tuthill, Abram Tuthill. Proved 9 Nov. 1796 by Abraham Tuthill. Administration granted 9 Nov. 1796 to Nathaniel King, Daniel Tuthill, Christopher Brown.

A-464. EDWARD PENNY, (probably of Southold) 23 Oct. 1796 ... gives grandson Benjamin Penny whole estate and to pay Abraham Corey Jr. 50 pounds ... executors: Benjamin Penny ... witnesses: Joseph Glover, Joseph Glover Jr., James W. Booth. Proved 9 Nov. 1796 by Joseph Glover Jr. Administration granted 9 Nov. 1796 to Benjamin Penny.

A-466. LAWRENCE PETERSON, of Brookhaven, 11 June 1796 ... gives poor of the town five pounds ... gives brother Olowf Peterson, cityson in Copenhagen, Denmark, remaining money ... executors: William Phillips, David Davie Jr. ... signed Lorrence Peterson ... witnesses: Ebenezer Homan, William Smith, William Turner. Proved 5 July 1796 by Ebenezer Homan and William Turner. Administration granted 5 July1796 to William Phillips and David Davis Jr.

A-467. HANNAH SMITH, of Huntington, 7 Jan. 1794 ... gives Frederick, son of daughter Susannah, five pounds ... gives daughter Susanna furniture ... gives son Jacob Smith third of remainder ... mentions what may be due from late brother Matthew Bunce's estate ... gives son Hezekiah Smith and daughter Abigail Johnson and daughter Susanna Smith two thirds equally divided ... executor: son Jacob Smith ... witnesses: Henry Scudder, Young P. Scudder, Henry Scudder Jr. Proved 16 Nov. 1796 by Young P. Scudder of Huntington. Administration granted 16 Nov.1796 to Jacob Smith.

A-469. JOHN ROBINSON, of Brookhaven, 9 June 1779 ... gives wife Elisabeth Robinson 50 pounds and five pounds a year ... gives two granddaughters Elizabeth and Martha Hopkins 200 pounds each ... gives son John Robinson 100 pounds and land in Ulster County, N.Y. ... .gives son Richard Robinson land and residue ... executor: son Richard Robinson ... witnesses: John Woodhull Jr., Wessell Sell, James Woodhull. Proved 6 Jan. 1797 by Wessell Sell. Administration granted 6 Jan. 1797 to Richard Robinson.

A-472. RICHARD STEER HUBBARD, of Southold, 30 Aug. 1765 ... gives wife Esther Hubbard whole estate ... executrix: wife Esther Hubbard ... witnesses: Joseph Hinchman, Nehemiah Barker, Theophilus Clark. Proved 17 Feb. 1797 by John Corwin and John Corwin Jr. who testified to handwriting of testator and of Nehemiah Barker (apparently also dead). Administration granted 17 Feb. 1797 to wife Esther Hubbard.

A-474. DAVID TOPPING, of Southampton, 7 Sept. 1796 ... gives wife Jane Topping 10 pounds ... gives daughter Phebe Dayton 60 pounds ... gives son Daniel Topping land ... gives son Matthew Topping land bought of Daniel and Jedediah Peirso (Pierson?) ... executors: two sons Daniel and Matthew Topping, and Daniel Howell ... witnesses: Ezekiel Howell, Price Howell, Stephen Howell. Proved 25 Feb. 1797 by Ezekiel Howell and Price Howell. Administration granted 25 Feb. 1797 to Matthew Topping and Daniel Howell.

A-476. ANNANIAS COOPER, of Southampton, 2 Aug. 1796.. gives daughter Mary Cooper 100 pounds and home while single, also land bought of Dr. Hallsey ... gives daughter Prudence Sayre 100 pounds ... gives daughter Phebe Parker 10 pounds ... gives grandson James Parker 80 pounds and interest when 21 ... if he dies before then his mother Phebe Parker and his sister Maria Parker to divide it ... gives granddaughter Maria Parker 10 pounds with interest when 18 ... gives granddaughter Polly Sayre a bed ... gives grandson Jared Cooke five pounds when 21 ... gives son Matthew Cooper land adjoining that of Samuel Howell, Paul Halsey, Benjamin Woodruff ... gives son Annanias Cooper land formerly father's, and land adjoining that of John Cook ... executors: friend Samuel Howell and sons Matthew and Annanias Cooper and James Sayre ... witnesses: Joseph Jacobs, Stephen Halsey Jr., Samuel H. Rose. Proved 25 Feb. 1797 by Joseph Jacobs "cordwainer." Administration granted 25 Feb. 1797 to Annanias Cooper and James Sayre.

A-479. JOHN BISHOP, of Southampton, 5 Feb. 1791 ... gives son Samuel Bishop land adjoining that of Mr. Sayre, Wilmun Hallsey, and land at Canoe Place ... gives son John Bishop Jr. land ... gives grandson Francis Bishop half ready cash ... gives daughter Mercy Bishop 10 pounds and home while single ... all other moveables equally divided between children Sarah Post, Mehitable Post, John Bishop, Samuel Bishop, Ann Seward, Susannah Jagger and Mercy Bishop ... executors: two sons John and Samuel Bishop ... witnesses: Jeremiah Post, Samuel Post, Joseph Goldsmith. Proved 25 Feb. 1797 by Jeremiah Post. Administration granted 25 Feb. 1797 to Samuel Bishop.

A-481. JONATHAN HALSEY of Southampton, 2 Dec. 1796 ... gives daughter Jane Halsey 40 pounds ... gives daughter Mehitable Halsey 40 pounds ... gives daughter, Permele Halsey 26 pounds ... gives daughter Susannah Halsey 25 pounds ... gives daughter Mary Bower five pounds ... gives son William Halsey 10 pounds ... gives son Hezekiah Halsey two pounds and blacksmith shop ... gives son George Halsey 10 pounds ... gives two sons David and Jonathan Halsey whole estate ... gives daughters Jane, Mehitable, Permele and Susana a home while single ... executors: sons David and Jonathan Halsey ... witnesses: David Halsey Jr., Caleb Halsey, Jonathan Rogers. Proved 25 Feb. 1797 by David Halsey Jr. and Caleb Halsey. Administration granted 25 Feb. 1797 to Jonathan Halsey.

A-464. JOHN EDWARDS, of Southampton, 15 Mar. 1794 ... provides for wife Mehetable Edwards ... gives son John Edwards five shillings and use of land adjoining that of Silas Stewart, which is to go at his death to grandsons Isaac and John Edwards ... gives son Silas Edwards five shillings and use of land adjoining that of Zacharias Sandford, which is to go to grandson Silas and grandson Thomas Edwards ... gives daughters Anne Edwards and Phebe Corry 10 pounds each

... gives two daughters Jemimah Crook and Lucretia Drake 10 pounds each ... executors: wife Mehitable and Samuel L'Hommedieu ... witnesses: Silas Stewart, Josiah Hand, Elias Matthews. Proved 25 Feb. 1797 by Josiah Hand. Administration granted 25 Feb. 1797 to Mehitable Edwards.

A-486. THOMAS ROBINSON, of Huntington, innkeeper, 11 Mar. 1797 ... "attacked 6 Mar. 1797 with a nervous complaint by means of which he was deprived of all rational sense until 11 Mar. 1797" a short time before his death ... gives all personal estate to Alexander, Phebe, Elisabeth, John and Mary, children of Elizabeth Soper, Alexander and John to have 50 pounds more than the girls ... witnesses: Amos Willets Jr., Amos Soper, Platt Vail Jr., David Driggs, Juliana Jarvis. Proved 31 Mar. 1797 by Amos Willets Jr., Amos Loper and Platt Vail Jr. Administration granted 31 Mar. 1797 to Israel Carll and Zebulon Buffet of Huntington.

A-488. TIMOTHY MILLER, of Brookhaven, 23 Jan. 1790... gives oldest daughter Deliverance 50 pounds ... gives oldest son Nathaniel land bought of Widow Rachel D'Houneur, land adjoining that of Mr. Hopkons, and land formerly of Richard Miller ... gives two sons Timothy and Joseph land adjoining that of Isaac Miller, Sarah Woodhull ... gives three daughters Joanna, Kiturah and Betsy 100 pounds each and home while single ... gives son Zophar land, 85 pounds and home until married ... mentions son Timothy is also unmarried ... "that which father-in-law Joseph Davis leaves me at his death I give to four daughters" equally ... sons Timothy and Joseph to pay daughter Deliverance 50 pounds ...executors: four sons Nathaniel, Timothy, Joseph and Zophar ... witnesses: Isaac Miller, Solon Halsey, Elisabeth Miller. Proved 4 Apr. 1797 by Isaac Miller. Administration granted 4 Apr. 1797 to Timothy and Zophar Miller.

A-492. SILAS COOPER, of Southampton, 23 Feb. 1797 ... provides for wife Elizabeth Cooper ... estate to be equally divided between children ... executor: friend Jonathan Rogers ... witnesses: David Cooper, Sarah Rogers, David Hodges. Proved 5 :May 1797 by Sarah Rogers. Administration granted 9 May 1797 to Jonathan Rogers.

A-493. URIAH MILLER, of Easthampton, 4 June 1790 ... provides for wife ... gives son Uriah land at Sag Harbor ... gives daughter Rachel while widow, home ... gives son Joel five shillings ... gives son Abraham five shillings ... gives three daughters Joanna, Phebe and Rachel four pounds ... gives son Nathan remainder of estate..,.executors: wife, son Nathan, and son-in-law Abraham Baker ... witnesses: Abraham Baker, Abraham Sherril, John Stratton. Proved 9 May 1797 by Abraham Baker. Administration granted 9 May. 1797 to Mrs. Miller, Nathan Miller, and Abraham Mulford.

A-495. PETER DAINS, of Southold, 31 Jan. 1797.. gives grandsons Peters Dains and Thomas Dains land at Riverhead ... their sister to have home until married ... gives daughter Mary and daughter Sarah 20 pounds each ... gives daughter Abigail 50 pounds and home while single ... gives son Samuel Dains land ... executors: sons Samuel and Timothy Dains, and friend Giles Wells ... witnesses: Sylvester Lester, Jonathan Horton, Bethiah Terry. Proved 31 May 1797 by Sylvester Lester. Administration granted 31 May 1797 to Giles Wells.

A-495.* DAVID LUPTON. of Southampton, blacksmith, (on file but not probated or indexed though it bears the inscription "David Luptons will probate issued 25 July 1797). 13 Mar. 1796 ... gives son David Lupton land ... gives two daughters Abigail Sayre and Keturah Vance five pounds each ... gives daughter Rebeckah Lupton 15 Pounds ... executor: son David Lupton ... witnesses: Mary Cooper, Ananias Cooper Jr., Anthony Ludlam.

A-497. ABIJAH OWEN, of Brookhaven, 29 Jan. 1796 ... provides for wife Elizabeth Owen ... remainder to four children John Owen, James Owen, Elizabeth Owen and brother Micah Owen when of age ... executors: wife Elizabeth Owen and brother Micah Owen ... witnesses; David Rose, Jonathan Webb, Christopher Mogar. Proved 2 Aug.1797 by the Rev. David Rose. Administration granted 2 Aug. 1797 to Micah Owen.

A-498. ISRAEL HAWKINS of Brookhaven, farmer, 20 June I'?82. gives wife Phebe 50 pounds ... gives daughters Ruth and Rebecca 50 pounds each ... gives daughter Susanna 40 pounds

and negress Dawn ... gives sons Israel and Nehemiah land ...
executors to be guardians of children until of age or married, and
of whole estate until son Israel is 21 ... executors: cousins
Alexander Hawkins Jr.,and Joseph Brewster, and brother-in-law
Phillips Roe ... witnesses: Jonathan Thompson, Phebe Wickes,
Samuel Thompson. Proved 18 Aug. 1797 by Samuel Thompson
"physician." Administration granted 13 Aug. 1797 to Phillips Roe.

A-501 SAMUEL PHILLIPS, of Brookhaven, very sick, 10 Apr.
1797 ... gives daughter Amy 10 shillings ... gives daughter
Charity 10 shillings ... gives son Fradrick 20 shillings ... gives
daughter Temperance moveables ... gives son Samuel
moveables ... executors: son Samuel Phillips and Timothy Davis
... witnesses: Joshua Davis, John Moger. Proved 4 Sept. 1797
by both Timothy and Joshua Davis. Administration granted 4
Sept. 1797 to Samuel Phillips.

A-503. JOSEPH GOLDSMITH, of Southampton, 26 Aug. 1797.
.. Gives wife Catharine Goldsmith five pounds ... gives two
daughters Mary and Catharine five shillings each ... estate to be
sold ... remainder to daughter Hannah ... executors: friend
Jonathan Rogers and daughter Hannah Goldsmith ... witnesses:
Daniel Sandford, Walter Rowell, John Reynolds. Proved 14
Sept. 1797 by Daniel Sandford and John Reynolds.
Administration granted 14 Sept. 1797 to Jonathan Rogers and
Hannah Goldsmith.

A-504. CONSTANT HAVINS, of Southampton, 8 1797 ... gives
daughter Abigail Jennings 20 shillings ... gives daughters
Lucretia, Peggy, Jerusha, Hannah, Polly and Nancy 30 pounds
each ... gives daughter Jerusha Hulbut a bed ... gives son
Constant 100 pounds ... gives son Jeremiah 100 pounds ...
gives son Biram land bought of Hugh Gelston Jr ... gives son
David 200 pounds ... gives son Gordon 200 pounds ... gives wife
Temperance 50 pounds ... gives daughter Hannah home with
her brother Biram while single ... executors: wife Temperance,
son Biram and friend Hugh Gelston Jr .... witnesses: Jonathan
Havens, Henry Corwithy, Bethiah Post. Proved 14 Sept. 1797 by
Bethiah Post. Administration granted 14 Sept . 1797 to
Temperance Havins and Hugh Gelston Jr.

A-507. ZEPHANIAH ROGERS, of Southampton, 28 Nov. 1792. ... -gives wife Elisabeth 20 pounds ... gives son Herrick moveables ... gives four daughters Susanna, Mary, Abigail and Hannah 35 pounds each and home while single ... gives daughter Huldah Sayre five pounds ... reminder of estate to be sold ... remainder gives to son Herrick Rogers ... executors: wife Elizabeth, son-in-law Thomas Sayre, and William Herrick .. . witnesses Zebulon Howell, Obadiah Wright, Merit Sayre. Proved 15 Sept. 1797 by Zebulon Howell. Administration granted 15 Sept. 1797 to William Herrick, and Mrs. Elizabeth Rogers.

A-509. JOEL SANDFORD, of Southampton, 24 Dec. 1796 ... gives wife furniture that her father left her ... gives children of son James Sandford one pound each. ... gives son Elihu 10 shillings ... gives son Lemuel half land ... gives son Jared 10 pounds ... gives son Oliver half land.. gives children of daughter Hamultal 20 shillings each ... gives daughter Prudence 50 pounds and home ... executors: sons Lemuel and Oliver ... witnesses: Jeremiah Ludlum, Caleb Hallsey, Fanny Ludlum. Proved 14 Sept. 1797 by Jeremiah Ludlum and Caleb Hallsey. Administration granted 14 Sept. 1797 to Lemuel Sandford.

A-510. RUTH HOWELL, of Easthampton, spinster, 18 June 1788 ... gives niece Ruth Hodges 60 pounds ... gives friend and kinswoman Phebe, wife of Samuel Isaac, a clock ... gives niece Elizabeth Jones 20 pounds ... gives sister Marry Isaacs the remainder ... executors sister Mary Isaac and nephew Isaac Isaacs ... witnesses: Josiah Mulford, Elizabeth Mulford, Samuel Hutchinson. Proved 14 Sept. 1797 by Elizabeth Mulford. Administration granted 14 Sept. 1797, when executors relinquished it, to Aaron Isaacs of Easthampton, brother-in-law to Ruth Howell, widow.

A-512. JOSEPH UDALL, of Islip, 22 Oct. 1797 ... provides for wife Phebe Udall ... at her death estate to be sold ... gives daughter Deborah Willets interest on 500 pounds while a widow ... then to children she now has ... gives daughter Sarah Jackson 500 pounds ... gives son Richard Udall 600 pounds, equivalent to what has been given other sons ... remainder divides as follows: quarter to Richard Udall, quarter to Daniel Udall, quarter to William Udall and quarter to Thomas Udalls (deceased) children Richard, Charles and Sarah Udall as they come of age .... executors: three sons Richard, Daniel and William Udall and son-in-law Jacob Seaman ... witnesses: Nehemiah Higbie, Jonah Willets, Prudence Carll. Proved 11 Jan. 1793 by Nehemiah Higbie of Islip. Administration granted 11 Jan. 1798 to Richard Udall.

A-515. MICAH SMITH, of Smithtown, 29 June 1797 ... gives son Jonas land, negroes Charles and Isaac ... gives daughters and daughter Charity's children moveables ... executors: son Jonas and two brothers-in-law Richard Smith and Nathaniel Smith ... witnesses: Caleb Smith, Joshua Smith, Rachel Wickes. Proved 5 Feb.1798 by Caleb and Joshua Smith of Smithtown. Administration granted 5 Feb. 1798 to Jonas Smith and Nathaniel Smith.

A-516. LEMUEL HALSEY, of Southampton, 22 Nov. 1797 ... provides for wife Abigail ... gives two oldest daughter Sarah and Phebe 10 shillings each ... gives daughter Hannah furniture equal to what Phebe had when married ... gives daughter Polly furniture, 40 pounds and home while single ... gives son Jesse land which came from "my father" White by my wife ... gives son Charles White Halsey lands ... executrix: wife Abigail ... witnesses: Silas White. James White Jr.,James White. Proved 23 Feb. 1798 by Silas and James White Jr. Administration granted 23 Feb. 1798 to Abigail Halsey.

A-518. DANIEL HODGES, of Southampton, 24 June 1794 ... gives wife 20 pounds ... gives grandson Daniel Hedges land at Winscot, bought of John Hoping, land adjoining that of David Hedges, land bought of Jeremiah Conkling in Easthampton, and of Ezekiel Hand ... gives son Abraham Hedges land adjoining John Dayton, Stephen Hedges ... gives son Caleb Hedges land had of Rusel ... gives son Nathaniel Hedges land adjoining Timothy Pierson, Hugh Gelston ... give sons Abraham and Caleb Hedges equally land at Montauk ... gives daughter Sarah Palmer eight pounds ... gives daughter Phebe Coock eight pounds ... gives daughter Hannah Pierson eight pounds ... gives daughter

Susannah Hedges 60 pounds ... gives daughter Martha Hedges 60 pounds ... gives granddaughter Abigail Hand five pounds ... executors: wife, Capt. David Pierson and son Abraham Hodges ... witnesses: David Hodges, Jesse Hedges. Peleg Pierson. Proved 22 Feb. 1798 by David Hodges of Southampton. Administration granted 22 Feb. 1798 to Mrs. Hedges, David Pierson, and Abraham Hedges.

A-521. ENSIGN NICKERSON, of Southampton, 9 Dec. 1797 ... executors to sell land and share in schooner "Prudent" ... gives daughter Alice her mother's things ... gives three daughters Alice, Tabitha and Abigail $150 ... gives wife Tabitha use of land until son James is of age ... gives son James remainder of estate ... executors: wife Tabitha and friend Joseph Crowell ... witnesses: Jonathan Havens, Samuel H. Rose, Samuel L'Hommediou. Proved 22 Feb. 1798 by Jonathan Havens of Southampton. Administration granted 22 Feb. 1798 to Joseph Crowell.

A-523. DAVID CORWITHE, of Southampton, 11 May 1795 ... gives son Burnet Corwithe use of land bought of David Schallinger, Ethan Halsey's executors, Daniel Moore. which at his death goes to grandson Burnet ... gives son Henry Corwithe land bought of David Hildreth, Arthur Howell, and share in Sag Harbor wharf ... gives son Caleb Corwithe lands ... gives grandson David Corwithe 200 pounds ... gives daughter Mary Gelston, Puah Gelston and Temperance Mitchell 100 pounds each ... gives daughter Sarah Parsons 50 pounds ... executors: two sons Henry and Caleb Corwithe ... witnesses: Elias Matthews, Elias Sandford, and Anna Brown. Proved 28 Feb. 1793 by Elias Sandford and Anna Brown, of Southampton. Administration granted 28 Feb. 1798 to Henry and Caleb Corwithe.

A-524. JOHN WILLETS, of Smithtown, 13 Jan. 1798. ..executors to sell estate ... gives father Amos Willets 30 pounds and interest on all money for life ... at his death estate goes to brother Samuel half, and to brother Isaac and sister Phibe half between them ... executors: brothers Isaac and Samuel, and brother-in-law Annin Mowbray ... witnesses: Silas Carll, Ananias

Carll, John Loper. Proved 13 Mar. 1798 by John Loper. Administration granted 13 Mar.1798 to Isaac and Samuel Willets.

A-525. JOHN WELLS, of Southold, 24 Jan. 1797 ... gives daughter Mary Wells, widow of Timothy Wells, deceased, land in St. George Manor, bought of Jeremiah Wells and and Jeremiah Petty, land bought of Parshall Howell at Broad Meadows ... gives grandson John Wells money owing from Timothy Wells, deceased, and money paid his sister Mary for her part of his father's estate ... gives daughter Abigail Goldsmith, wife of Joseph Hull Goldsmith, land bought of James Wells, John Benjamin, James Petty, at Aquebogue ... gives wife Mary 200 pounds ... gives daughter Hannah Wells 25 pounds ... gives two daughters Hannah Wells and Sarah Fleet land equally divided ... executors: son-in-law Joseph Hull Goldsmith and friend Jared Landon ... witnesses: Joshua Benjamin, Daniel Case. Simeon Benjamin. Proved 28 Mar. 1798 by Simeon Benjamin of Southold. Administration granted 28 Mar. 1798 to Joseph Hull Goldsmith and Jared London.

A-528. JONATHAN CORWIN of Riverhead, 26 July 1723 ... gives son Selah land ... gives daughter Hannah Goodale land In Southampton ... gives son Lea Corwin remaining land ... gives grandson Jason Corwin 100 pounds at 21 ... gives wife 20 pounds ... executors: sons Selah and Asa Corwin ... witnesses: John Hubbard, Joseph Parker Wickham. Codicil 24 July 1797 ... witnesses: Joseph Parker Wickham, Jacob Rickhow, Phebe Wickham. Proved 19 Apr. 1798 by Joseph Parker Wickham. Administration granted 15 Apr. 1798 to Selah and Asa Corwin.

A-530. JOHN BUNCE, of Huntington, 9 Mar. 1798 ... gives two grandchildren Jesse Bunce Scribner and Luri Scribner five shillings each ... gives son Thomas apparel ... gives four sons Thomas, John Jiffery and Elkanah Bunce land equally divided ... executors: two sons Thomas and Jeffery Dunce ... witnesses: Jeremiah Smith, Henry Scudder Jr., Henry Scudder. Proved 2 May 1798 by Henry Scudder Jr. Administration granted 2 May 1798 to Thomas and Jeffery Bunco.

A-532. AME BRUSH, of Huntington, 2 May 1795 ... gives Ame Smith, daughter of John Smith, whole estate and money from estate of Daniel Brush, deceased, late husband ... but should Ame Smith die under 18, estate goes to Mary Brush, daughter of Jacamiah Brush ... executors: friends John Oakley and Jacamiah Brush ... witnesses: Richard Brush, Edward Brush. Proved 13 June 1798 by Edward Brush. Administration granted 13 June 1798 to John Oakley and Jacamiah Brush.

A-534. JOSEPH ROGERS, of Southampton, I July 1798 ... gives wife provisions ... gives son Job Rogers 10 shillings ... gives son Jesse Rogers land adjoining that of Jonathan Hallsey ... gives son Joseph Rogers land in Topping Purchase in Quague ... gives daughter Jerusha Tuthill five shillings ... gives daughter Jerusha Rogers five shillings ... gives daughter Rachel Rogers five shillings ... executors: wife Sarah Rogers, Josiah Phillips and son Jesse Rogers ... witnesses: Josiah Rayner, Jeremiah Culver, Jonathan Halsey. Proved 13 July 1798 by Jeremiah Culver of Southampton. Administration granted 13 July 1798 to son Jesse Rogers.

END OF LIBER A.

A-107* ZEBULON ROBBINS, of Brookhaven, 4 Oct. 1784 (on file but not recorded and indexed) ... provides for wife Susannah ... gives brother-in-law Robert Jayne 300 pounds ... gives Daniel Robbins, son of nephew Isaac Robbins, reminder of estate ... executors: wife Susannah Robbins, brother-in-law Robert Jayne, nephew Isaac Robbins ... witnesses: Cyrus Punderson, Morris Jayne, Sarah Jayne. Proved 9 Apr. 1789 by Sarah Jayne of Brookhaven, and 10 Apr. 1789 by Morris Jayne of Smithtown.

INDEX OF PERSONS

This exhaustive index to every personal name mentioned in the wills was prepared by Mr. Easter nearly 70 years ago. The "A" numerals refer to the will numbers in the text and NOT to pages. The number in parentheses () following some will numbers are to his count of people of same name mentioned in the same will. This immense labor must have been done in the old fashioned way, either on handwritten slips or cards that were then sorted by hand. The serious researcher should be grateful to Easter for all this effort. A simple index to surnames only would have saved most of this drudgery, plus an enormous number of hours spent in typing.

His treatment of variant spellings varies. For some surnames individuals of obviously the same family (but with different spellings) are lumped together. In other cases really similar family names are indexed exactly as written. It may be that his knowledge of certain early Suffolk County families made these decisions simple and important.

This digitized copy of his book has been done by feeding the tiny, tiny pages of the original typed book (on what is now decayed and discolored newspaper stock) through a scanner into WordPerfect 7. The transfer was far from perfect, and the printout was compared page by page to the original. The numerals in the index were much harder to correct, and it may be taken as certain that some errors (hopefully only a few) remain in the digitized copy. If the reader runs into a blind reference in the index, variant will numbers should be checked. The scanner occasionally had problems differentiating between 2/3, 5/6, and 3/8 when lightly typed or smudged.

Abbet, Stephen A420 (3)
Akerly, Abel A295 (2)
　Charity A251
　Mrs. Dority A251
　Mrs. Dowryty A251
　Elijah A251
　Gilbert AI95
　John A157 (2), AI80 (2)
　Martha A251
　NATHANIEL A229, A251
　Platt AI49 (2)
　Robert A374
　Ruth A251
　Stephen A251
Akly, Gilbert A195
Alben, Ebenezer A349
Arden, James A450 (2)
Arthur, Platt A229
Avery, HUMPHREY AI54 (6)
　Mary AI54
　Nathan AI54
　Roger AI54 (4)
　Solomon AI54
　Susanna AI54
　Thomas AI54 (4)
Ayre, Mrs. Jemima A282
Babbit, Mrs.Eunice AI27
Baker, Abraham A493 (2)
　Daniel A354
　Mrs.Mehitabel A48
Barker, Nehemiah A472 (2)
Barnes, Abraham A7 (2), A354
　Noah A328
Baron, Hannah A50
　Mary A50
Barto, Morris A341
Bayard, Samuel Jr. AI82
Bayley, Mehetabel A9

Beale, Hannah A90
　Matthew A2, A92
Bebee, Mrs. Anna A399
Bend, Grove A105 (2)
Benjamin, Isaiah A460
　John A525
　Joshua A90 (2), A525
　Nathan A90
　Simeon A525 (2)
　William A312
Bennet, Ame AI32
　Widow A73
Bennett, John AI7
Bigelow, Mrs.Hannah A253
Biggs, Abel A448 (2)
　Deborah A448
　ISAAC A290
　Isaac Smith A290 (3)
　Mrs. Mary A290
　Nathaniel A428 (2)
　Ruth A290 (2)
Bishop, Abigail A39, A424
　Francis A479
　George A236 (2)
　Harry A425 (2)
　Hennery A39
　Henry A39, A424 (3)
　Jemima A39 (2), 424 (2)
　JAMES A39 (2), A236, A424
　JOHN A39, A424 (4), A458, A479 (4)
　John Jr. A479
　Jonah A39, W424 (4)
　Mrs. Mahitable A452
　Mercy A479 (2)
　Samuel A479 (4)
　Sarah A90
　Stephan AI43, A236, A330

Mrs.Susanna A39, A236 (3)
Blackly, Moses A347
  Pene (Penelope?) A347 (2)
Blydenburgh, Richard A339
  William A339 (2), A434
Booth, Austin A282
  Catie Maria A382
  Constant Al64, A382 (2)
  Mrs.Elizabethh A382 (3)
  Fanny A382
  Henry A382
  James W. A372 (2), A429 (2) A464
  James Wheelock A69 (2)
  Al91 (2)
  JOSEPH A282 (2), A382 (2)
  Joshua Hobart A372
  Katie Maria A382
  Victor A382
  William Al60
  William Actin A382 (2)
Bowditch, Williiam A27 (2)
Bower, Mrs. Mary A481
Brasier, Elisabeth A424
Brewster, Benjamin A289
  Charles Jeffery A374 (2)
  Mrs. Hannah A227
  Isaac A289 (2)
  Joseph A217 (2), A498
  Mrs. Martha A426
  Mrs. Temperence A289
  WILLIAM A289
Broome, Betsy A273
  Caroline A273
  George Washington A273
  Henrietta A273
  Horatio Gates A273
  Jennet A273

Mary Platt A273
Mrs. Phobe A273
Samuel A273
Samuel Platt A273
Brown, Abigail A423
  Anna Al56, A523 (2)
  Christopher A447, A462 (2)
  Daniel A423 (2)
  David A423
  Deborah A92
  Mrs. Desire A92
  Elizabeth A64
  Isaac A423
  JAMES A64
  Mrs.James A64
  Joseph A423
  Mary A64
  Phillips A432
  Reubin A92
  Mrs. Rhoda A282
  Richard A92 (5), Al72 (2), A447
  Samuel A64
  Sarah A64
Browne, Elizabeth A64
  JAMES A64
  Mrs.James A64
  Mary A64
  Samuel A64
  Sarah A64
Brundage, Jesse A76 (2)
Brush, Mrs. AME A532
  ANANIAS A341
  Benjamin A456 (2)
  Daniel A34 (2), A532
  Ebenezer A406
  Ebenezer B. A406
  Edward A532 (2)
  Mrs.Elizabeth A34, A57
  EZEKIEL A456

82

Fanny A406 (2)
Freelove 406 (2)
Hebsibah A34 (2)
Ichabod A406
Jacamiah A34 Al 72 (2), A205 (2) A341 (2), A456 (5), A532 (3)
James A456 (2)
Jesse A406 (2)
JOHN A341, A406 (6)
JONATHAN A34
Joshua A34 (2), A320
Josuit A34 (2)
Mrs.Judith A341 (2)
Mrs.Margaret A320
Mary A532
Mrs. Mary A456
Nathan A341
Rebecca A406
Richard A456 (2), A532
Robert A34 (3)
Samuel A428 (2)
Samuel Scudder A406 (2)
Mrs.Sarah A55
Smith A34 (3), A428
Stephen A341
Zophar A341 (3), A456
Bryan, Alexander Al 14, A344
Augustine A59
Azel Al14 (2), Al 69
Ebenezer A344
Elisabeth A344
Mrs.Elizabeth A344
EPENETUS Al14, Al69
Jacob Al69
Jemima A344
Jesse A39 (2), Al14 (3), A344
John Al14
LEMUEL Al14 (3), A344

Melancthon A36, A59, Al14, A344
Nathaniel Al14
Mrs.Rhoda Al14, Al56, Al69
Smith A344
Stratton Al14
Trulove A344
Widow A59
Buchanan, Clarinda A27
Buell, Mrs.Mary A354
Buffet, Isaac Al 92 (2), A367 (2)
John A34 (2), A247
Mrs. Sarah A59, A203
Zebulon A347 (2),A486
Bunc, Joseph A20
Bunce, Abigail A295
Eliphalet A80, A344
Elisabeth (Brasier) A424
Elkannah A530
Gorge (George) A293
Hannah A293. A467
Jiffery A530 (3)
JOHN A530 (2)
Joseph A20
Joshua A293
Lemuel A293
MATHEW A293 (2), A467
Nathaniel Al5 (2), Al56 (3), Al69 (2), A229
Samuel A344, A424 (2)
Mrs. Sarah A293
Thomas A530 (4)
Burnet, Mrs. Arrezine Al
David Al19
Joseph Al (2)
Burr, Isaac A428
Burtis, Malby A456
Bushop, Sarah A90
Bushup, Mrs. Mahitable A452

Campbell, Angus AI67
Canef, Mrs. Phebe A57
Carll, Ananias A59 (3), A80
   (2), A524
   Mrs. Eelse A229
   Eliphalet A229
   Mrs. Hannah A59
   Israel A247, A406
   Mrs. Jerusha A59
   Prudence A512
   Mrs. Ruth A339
   Mrs. Sarah A416
   Silas A369, A524
   Timothy A59 (3), A339
Carman, Elizabeth A55
   Mrs. Elizabeth A203
   Mrs. Gean A455
   Mrs. Jean A318 (2)
   JOHN A55 (4), A318 (2),
   A455 (3)
   Samuel A55 (3)
Carmon, Mrs. Elizabeth A203
Carpenter, Mrs. Elizabeth AI76
Case, Abigail A429
   Anne A429
   BENJAMIN A67 (3)
   Daniel A67, A525
   Mrs. Esther A67
   Eunice A147 (2)
   Gershom A67 (2)
   Gilbert A67
   Ichabod A67
   James A429 (3)
   Prudence A429
   WILLIAM A429
Cells, Mrs. Jemima AI14
Chatfield, Henry A211 (2),
   A354 (2)
   John A7 (2), AI82 (2), A211
   (3),A354 (2)

Chichester, Eliphalet A456
   Mrs. Margaret A55
Chipman, Ward AI05
Church, Carolina AI07
Clark, Anna A402
   Benjamin A90
   Bethsheba AI03 (2)
   Cornelius A217 (2)
   Deborah AI03
   Deliverance AI03 (2)
   Hannah AI03 (3)
   John A265
   JOSHUA A90
   Mary AI03 (2)
   Mrs. Molly A90 (3)
   Oliver A63 (2)
   Mrs.Phebe AI03
   Puah AI03 (2)
   Samuel A190 (2)
   Samuel L. A90 (3)
   Theophilus A472
   WILLIAM AI03 (3)
   Mrs. William Sr. AI03
Clarkson, Catharine A441
Clayton, Samuel A450
Cleveland, Abigail A323
   Anna A323
   Benjamin A323 (3)
   JOSEPH A323 (4)
   Lazarus A323 (3)
   Mary A323
   Mrs.Mary A323
   Mehetable A323
Cleves, Daniel AI96 (2)
   David A426
   Experience AI96
   Jemima AI96
   JOSHUA AI96 (2)
   Mary A90, AI96
   Mrs. Mehetable AI96

Phebe Al96
Close, John A293
Coddington, Benjamin A408
Colbum, Josiah A89
Colden, Cadwallader Al82
Cole, Thaddeus Al86 (2)
Colwell, Jacob A78
Colyar, Mrs. Sarah A45
Comstock, Daniel A432 (2),
    A439 (2)
Conkling, Abigail A300
    Ananias Al72 (2)
    Mrs. Azubah Al52
    Benjamin A27
    Beuel A43
    Daniel Al64 (3), A300
    DAVID A41 (2), Al96 (4),
    A223,
    A261(2),A265(2),A280(2),A
    310, A316, A362, A445(3)
    Mrs.Deborah A303
    Edward A303
    Eleazar A7
    Eliazer A300
    Elishia A7
    Elizabeth A43, A87
    ELKANA Al74 (3)
    Enoch A43
    Epenetus Al74 (3), A206,
    A,413
    Ezekiel A316 (3)
    Gamaliel A41
    Henry A43, A303
    Hibbard A273
    Hubbard A316
    Jacob A41 (3), Al74 (2)
    Jemima A43
    Jeremiah Al64, A354, A518
    JESSE Al52 (3)
    John A41

John Carman Al 74
Jonathan A87
Jonathan Stratton A300 (2)
Mrs. Lida A377
Lineus A300
Martha A90
Mary A, 174, A300
Mrs. Mary A, 174
Mulford A300
Nathan Al64, A300
NATHAN Jr. A48, A87
Mrs. Phebe A341
Phillip A273, A316
Platt Al74
Rebacca A43, Al67
RICHARD A43, A205 (2)
Mrs. Ricbard A43
Mrs. Ruth A247
Samuel Al64, A300
Sarah A223
Selah A205 (2), A293 (2)
Stephen A41 (2)
THOMAS A167, A316
THOMAS SR A,316
Titus A43 (2)
Cook, Abraham A328
    Mrs. Anna A352
    Mrs. Carolina Al76
    ELIAS A305
    Esther A287
    Henry A305 (3)
    Jared A476
    John A53 (2), Al76, A305,
    A399, A476
    Mrs. Mehetabel A308
    Mrs. Phebe A518
    Proculah A53 (2)
    Silas A443
    Stephen A305 (4), A399
    William A305, A450

Cooke, Jared A476
Cooper, Abigail Jr. A263
ANNANIAS A476 (4)
Annanias Jr. A495
Caleb A32 (4), AI23 (2),
AI45, A200 (2) A263
Clarissa A32
David A492
Elizabeth A32 (2)
Mrs. Elizabeth A492
Hannah A328
John A32 (2)
Josiah A52 (2), A328 (2),
A399
Mary A452, A476, A495
Matthew A476 (2)
Matthew H. A399 (2)
Obadiah A123 (2)
Samuel A441
SILAS A386, A492
Mrs. SUSANNAH A32
Thomas A32 (2), AI76
Zophar A263 (2)
Cornish, Elkanah A243
Corry, Mrs. Phobe A484 (see
Cova)
Corvell, Joshua A76
Corwin, Amaziah AI78 (2),
A265 (3)
Asa AI37, A528 (3)
David AI37 (2)
Ezra A362 (2)
Henry A216
Jason A528
Jeremiah A216 (2)
John A472
John Jr. A472
Jonathan A528
Mrs. Jonathan A528
Joseph AI78 (2)

Mary A315
Mrs. Mary A265 (3)
Mary Jr. A315
Sarah A265
Selah A528 (3)
Thomas A265 (2)
TIMOTHY A265 (5)
Corwithe, Ann A305
Corwithy, Burnet A523 (2)
Corwethe, Caleb A396, A523
(3)
DAVID A305, A399, A523
(2)
Henry A269, A504 A523 (3)
Mrs. Katurah A305
Mary A305
Permele A305
Cova (Corey?), Abrahem Jr.
A464
Covert, Mrs. Catherine A76
Gorg (George) A458 (2)
Jacob A76
Crook, Mrs. Jemimah A484
Crowell, Joseph A521 (2)
Culver, Edward AI23
Jeremiah AI23, A534 (2)
JESSE A123
Mehatabel AI23
Moses AI23 (3)
Mrs. Phebe AI23
Zephaniah AI23
Curtis, John A73 AI32, A217
(3), A357
A419 (2)
Malby (Burtis)
Dains, Abigail A495
Mary A495
PETER A495 (2)
Samuel A495 (2)
Sarah A495

86

Thomas A495
Timothy A495
Dallas, Charles Al07 (2) A217
Darling, Mrs. Catherine A410
   Hamilton A410 (2)
   Mrs. Ruth A410
Darow, Mrs. Susannah A293
Davids, Nathaniel A251 (2)
   Samuel A429 (2)
   Timothy A501 (3)
Davis, Abigail A448
   Benjamin Al91
   Caleb A357 (2)
   Caturah A448 (2)
   Charity A357 (2)
   David Jr. A466 (2)
   Elizabeth A357 (3)
   Issac A260 (2) A281 (2) A325
   James Al9 (2) A334
   John A50 (2)
   JONAS Al7 (2) A260 A357 (3)
   Joseph A488
   Joshua A501 (2)
Davis, Martba A448
   Mrs. Martha A448
   Mary A448
   Mrs. Mehetabel A377
   Nathaniel Al9, A97 (2), Al02 (2), Al34 (2) A334 (2)
   Nathaniel 2nd. A337
   Mrs. Puah A300
   Spuer A432
   STEPHEN A448
   Sybil A357 (2)
   Mrs. Tabitha A357 (3)
   Timothv A432 (2)
Day, David A453 (3)
Dayton, Daniel A300

Mrs. Hannah A303
HENRY A5, A303
Jesse A87 (2) Al98 (2)
John A518
Mrs. Phebe A474
Samuel A303 (3)
Decker, Mrs. Elizabeth A458
Deiker, Mrs. Elizabeth A458
De Lancies, Brig. Gen. Al67
Dering, Elizabeth A257
   Henry Packer A257
   Mrs. Mary A257 (3)
   Sylvester A257
   THOMAS A257
Dewick, Richard Al07 (2)
Dibbel, Sineus A182 (2)
Dickerson (see Dickinson)
   Alice A521 (2)
   Elisha A9 (2)
   Jonathan A73
   Samuel A9 (2)
   WILLIAM A447 (3)
Dickinson, Abigail A447
   Abraham 447
   Benjamin A447
   Bethiah A447
   David A447
   Elijah A447
   Elijah A447
   John A447
   Jonathan A325 (3) A447 (3)
   Joshua A325
   Mary A447
   Matthew (Matty?) A447
   Ruaner A447
   WILLIAM A447 (3)
Dinge, Esther A245
Dinges, Selah Al12 (2)
Dingy, Mrs. Ruth Al52

Diser, Margit A428
Dominy, Mr. A300
  Henry A276
  Nathaniel AI30 (2) AI47 (5),
  AI64 AI30 (2)
  Nathaniel Jr. AI30 (2)
Dow, Hannah A388
  JACOB A388
  Joseph A388 (5)
  Mrs. Phebe A388
  Phillip A388
  Samuel A388
  Thomas A388 (2)
Downs, Mrs. Abigail A377
  DAVID A280 (2) A310 (4)
  Elizabeth A31 0
  Mrs. Elizabeth A310 (3)
  Hannah A225 (2)
  JAMES A225 (3)
  Mrs. Mary A216 (3)
  Mehitable A225 (2)
  PETER A216 (2)
Drake, Mrs. Lucretia A484
Drigge, David A486
Dunton, Alexander A408 (2)
Early, John AI67
Edwards, Abrahan AI64
  Anna A484
  Daniel A296 (3)
  Daniel Jr. A296
  Isaac AI62 (2) A484
  JOHN A484 (3)
  Mrs.Mehetable A484 (3)
  Mrs. Sarah AI26
  Silas A484
  Stephen A328
  Thomas A484
Ellis, Joseph A25
Everitt, John AI 52
Fanning, Mrs. Anna A312

Daniel Wells A312
Davis A382 (2)
  Mrs. Mary A223 (2)
  PHINEAS A460
Fausters, Benjamin A443
Fields, Jame A300
Fithian, Aaron A300
  David A300
Fleet, Alexander AI92 (4) A195
  (2)
  Ann AI92 (2)
  Augustine A344
  Mrs. Deborah AI92
  Gilbert AI92
  JOHN A57 AI92 (2) AI95
  Joshua AI95
  Ransler AI95
  Rebekah AI92 (2)
  Sarah AI92 (2) A377 (2)
  Mrs. Sarah A525
  SIMON A67 A59 AI92
Flint, Mrs. Keziah AI26
Floyd, Col. A97
  Mrs.Hannah A263
  John A392 (2)
  Mary A257
  Nicoll A441
Fordham, Mrs. Hannah A127
  James AI27 A287 John
  A89 (2)
  Nathan A89 (2)
Foster, Mrs. Ann A238
  Benjamin A238 (3) A443
  Christopher A384
  DANIEL A227
  David A238
  David Haines A24 (2) A63
  (2) A66 (2) AI21 (2) A227
  (3)
  Hannah A66

Jabez A384
James A332
Jerusha A227
Josiah A238
Mrs. Marah AI27
Matthew A308 (2)
Nathan A240 (2)
Pamela A227
Peter A227 (2)
Rufus A227 (3)
Sarah A238
SILAS A66 AI27
Stephen A238 (3)
Mrs.Temperance A227
WILLIAM A238 (4) A263
Fournier, Deborah A92 (2)
Francois A92
Franks, John A282
Furman, Zebulon AI54 (2)
Gardiner, Abraham AI82 (2)
    A354
Benjamin A402 (3)
DAVID AI82 (2)
Elizabeth A402
Eunice A402
Fletcher A402
Hannah AI 82
James A402
Jared A402
Jeremiah A303 (2)
Jerusha AI82
Mrs. Jerusha AI82
Jeter A402
JOHN A300 A349 A402 (5)
John Jr. A383
John Lyon AI82
Lion AI89 (2)
Luther AI89
Mary A402
Nathaniel AI82

Samuel A303
Septimus AI82
Garson, Peter A369 (3)
Geilston. Hugh A25 (2)
    Malby A25
Gelston, Hugh A25 (2) AI43
    (2) A518
Hugh Jr. A269 (2) A504 (3)
John A64 (2) A222 (2)
    A269 A399
Malby A25 AI82 A443
Mrs. Mary A523
Mrs. Puah A523
Thomas A269 (2)
Garrard, Benjamin A419 (2)
Mrs. Elizabeth A419 (3)
Isaac A419 (2)
Mary A419 (2)
Nathaniel A419
STEPHEN A419
Gibbs, Daniel A336
Joseph A29 A71 A386
Gildersleeve, BENJAMIN A347
Elizabeth A241 (2)
Mrs. Elizabeth A241 A347
Fitch A347
John A347
Jonas A36 A347 (3)
Obadiah A384
Phillips A347
Thomas A347
Thomas White A39 (2)
Whitehead AI69 (2)
Glover, David A289
Jonah A296
Joseph A464
Joseph Jr. A464 (2)
Goldsmith, Abigail A377
Mrs Abigail A525
Benjamin A90 (2)

Betsey A236
Catharine A503
Mrs. Catherine A503
Daniel A372 (4)
Hannah A236 (2) A308 (2)
A503 (3)
Jeremiah Al80
John A66
JOSEPH A66 (2) A85 (2)
A236 (2) A308 A479 A503
Joseph H. A377
Joseph Hull A525 (3)
Mary A503
Phobe A315
ZACCHEUS A372
Gooale, Stephen A63
Goodale, Mrs. Hannah A528
Joseph A430 (2)
Stephen A63
Green, Jacob Al86
Polly A269
Grice, Charles Al69
Mrs. Mary Al14
Griffing, Nathaniel A265
Grindle, John A450
Griswold, Mrs. Achaah Al76
Haff, Sary A428 (3)
Hains, ANTHONY A278
Mrs.Anthony A278 (2)
Benjamin A278 (4)
Carolina A278
Daniel A396
David A85 (2) A365 (2)
A396 (3) A430 (2)
James A50 A396
Job A278 (2) A396
John A200 A278 (2)
Nathan A323
Pewer A278
Puah A276

SAMUEL A53 (2) A222
A396
Mrs. Sarah A396
Stephen A396 (3)
Temperance A278
Hair, Jared A305 (2)
Nathan A305
Silvinas A305
Hallicok, William A330 (2)
Hallock, Benjamin A362 (2)
Hannah A362 (2)
John A260
Jonathan A357
Lydia A362 (2)
Mary A362 (2)
Noah A334
Patience A362 (2)
Samuel A362 (2)
WILLIAM A362 (5)
Zebulon A296
Halloick, William A25 (2) A330
(2)
William R. A332 (2)
Hallsey, Capt. A435
Dr. A476
Mrs. Abigail A386 A516 (4)
Abraham A222
Asintha A52
Caleb A481 (2) A509 (2)
Mrs.Charity A386
Charles White A516
Clarissa A63
David A481 (2)
David Jr. A481 (2)
DAVID FITHIN A63 A227
Elisha A352 (2)
Ethan A523
Fithin A227
George A481
Hannah A516

90

Mrs. Hannah A145
Henry A63 A222 (2) A441
(2)
Hezekiah A481
Isaac A255 (2)
Jane A481
Jesse A85 (2) A386 (3)
A516
John Al23 A227
JONATHAN A263 A481 (4)
A534
LEMUEL A29 (2) A386 (5)
A516
Lucinda A63
Mary A52 A255
Mrs. Mary Al76
Mehitable A481
Pamela A481
Paul A253 A399 A476
Permale A481
Phebe A52 A516 (2)
Mrs. Phebe A52
Polly A63 A516
Mrs. Prudence A352
Sarah A269 A516
Mrs. Sarah A399
Silas A200 (2) A278 (2)
Silvanus A63 (2)
Solon A488
Stephen A253 A399
Stephen Jr. A476
Susan A200
Susannah A481
THEOPHILUS A52
Timothy A63
William A52 A399 A435 (2)
A481
Wilmun A479
Hammond, Elisha Al 57 (2)
Hand, Abigail A518

David A50
Elizabeth Al62
Ezeciel A518
Henry Dominies Al 98
John A384
Josiah A328 A484 (2)
Nathaniel Al62 (2)
Handspath, Stephen A7
Harris, Mrs.Abigail Al 21
Daniel Al21
David Al21 (4) A278
Elias Al21 A443 (2)
Mrs. Hannah A240
HENRY Al21 (5) A278
Jane Al21
John A200
Sarah Al21
Hart, John A90 (2)
Joshua A344 (2) A420
Micah Al74 (2)
Harvey, David A90 (2)
Hatch, Mrs. Hannah Al26
Havens, Augustus A27
Mrs. Bethiah A458
EBENEZER A27
James A27
Mrs. Jerusha A29
John Jr. A452 (3)
Jonathan A521 (2)
Joseph A27 (3)
Havins, Biram A504 (2)
CONSTANT A504 (2)
David A504
Gordon 1504
Hannah A504 (2)
Jeremiah A504
Jonathan A504
Lucretia A504
Nancy A504
Peggy A504

Polly A504
Mrs. Temperance A504 (3)
Hawkins, Allicksander A325
  Alexander Jr. A498
  Benjamin A426
  Daniel A334 A337
  Deborah A390 (2)
  ELEAZER A426
  ELIAZER A260 (3)
  Mrs. Eliazer A260 (2)
  Elizabeth A426
  Mrs. Elizabeth A434
Hawkins, Elnathan A426
  GEORG Al7
  ISRAEL A325 A498 (3)
  Jacob A426 (2)
  John A434
  Jonas A260 (3) A360 (2)
  AZ90 (2)
  Joseph Al7
  Joseph S. Al7 (2)
  Mary A426 (2)
  Mrs. Mary A426 (2) A434
  Nehemiah A498
  Mrs. Phebe A498
  Rebecca A498
  Ruth A390 (2) A498
  Mrs. Ruth Al7 (2)
  Susanna A498
  Thomas A290
  William Al7 (3) A434
Hedges, Abraham A518 (4)
  Caleb A518 (2)
  DANIEL A300 A328 A354
  A518 (2)
  Mrs. Daniel A518 (2)
  David A50 A394 (2) A492
  A518 (3)
  Ebenezer A300
  Elias Al59 (3) Al86 A354

  Elizabeth Al59 Al86
  Mrs. Elizabeth Al59 (3)
  EZEKIEL A5 Al59 Al86
  Mrs. Hannah Al86
  Jacob A87 (2)
  Jeremiah A384
  Jeriah Al59
  Jerusha Al86
  Jesse A518
  Mrs. Joanna Al86
  Joseph Al59 (5)
  Lemuel A354
  Martha A518
  Mrs. Mary A48
  Nathaniel A518
  Ruth A51 0
  Stephen A48 (2) A518
  Susannah A518
  William A300
Helme, Caleb A334 (2)
  Thomas A217 (3) A334
Helmes, Thomas A334
Hendrickson, Mrs. DORCUS
  Al56
  Mrs. Hannah Al74
Herrick, Abgil A25
  George A25
  Henry Al27 A261
  William A143 (2) A235
  A240 (2), A332 A443 A507
  (2)
Higbie Amos A388 (2)
  Daniel Al49
  Nathaniel Al49
  Nehemiah A512 (2)
Hildreth, David A623
  Isaac A399 (2)
  James A399
  JOHN A305 A399 (2)
  Joseph A443

Joshua A52 (2) A71 (2)
Luthur A399
Mrs. Mary A240
Mrs. Mehetable A29 A399
Peter A50
Polly A399
Septimus A399 (3)
Hill, Mrs. Mehetabel AI76
Hillock, Mrs. Phebe AI26
Hinchman, Joseph A472
Homan, Abigail A452
  Mrs.Anna AI87
  Catharine A452
  Ebenezer AI87 A466 (2)
  Elizabeth A452
  Mrs. Elizabeth A452
  Marah A452
  Mordecai A208 (2)
Hoping, John A518
Hopkins, Mr. A488
  Elizabeth A469
  Mrs. Elizabeth A337
  Martha A469
  Samuel A432 (2)
Horton, Anna A9 (2) A71 (2)
  BARNABUS A9 (3)
  Benjamin A9 (2) A323
  David A223
  Eunice A71 (3)
  Gilbert A9 (2)
  James A9
  Jonathan A9 A69 (3) A281
  A323 (2) A495
  Joshua A69
  Justus A9
  Lazarus A325
  Mrs. Mary A69
  Mehetable A69
  Micah A69
  Moses A69

Mrs. Patience A69
Phebe A69
Prudence A71 (3) A223
Rebecca A9 (2)
Mrs. Rebecca A9
Susan(na) A9 (2)
Mrs. Susanna A9
WILLIAM A69 (5) A402 (2)
Howell, Abigail A145
  Abraham A25 A50 (2) A443
  (2)
  Mrs. Anna AI21
  Arthur A523
  Charles A25 A443
  Cynthia A281 (2)
  Damaris A443
  Daniel AI26 (2) A330 A474
  (2)
  DAVID A25 (3) AI27 (2)
  A281 A305 A443 (4)
  David III A376 (2)
  Mrs. Deborah A71
  Ebenezer A235
  ELIAS A145 (4)
  Elizabeth A330 (2)
  Mrs. Elizabeth A330 A377
  Ephraim A65 (2) AI 27 (2)
  A287
  EZEKIEL A71 A328 A394
  (2) A474 (2
  Ezekiel Jr. A25
  Hannah A396
  Mrs. Hannah A29
  Henry A330
  James A235 A332
  Jerebel A25
  JOHN A235 (5) A281 (2)
  Jonah AI45
  Jonathan A281 (3) A362
  JONATHAN JR. A281

Joshua A328
LEMUEL AI27 (3) A287
Lucretia A235
Matthew A443 (3)
Matthew Jr. A25
Mehetabal AI27 A287
Moses A53 (2) A328
Nathan A235
OBADIAH A330 (2) A332
Pamelia A443
Parshal A525
Phebe A396
Mrs. Phebe A263 A441 A443
Phillip A305
Price AI26 (2) A474 (2)
Reeve AI3 (2)
RICHARD A330 A332
Ruth AI45
Mrs. RUTH A510 (2)
Ryall A332
SAMUEL A53 (2), AI27, A399 A476 (2)
Samuel Jr. A305 (2)
Sarah AI27
Mrs. Sarah AI27 (2)
SILAS A25 (4) A328 A443
Silvanus A25 (2) A332 (2)
Silvanus Jr. A305
Simon AI26
Stephen A25 (6) A235 (2) A443 (2)A474
Thomas A328
Walter A52 (2) A503
Zebulon A507 (2)
Hubbard, Bethiah A223
Mrs. Esther A472 (2)
John A9 AI78 (2) A223 (4) A528
Mrs. Mary A241

RICHARD STEER A472
Richard S. Jr. A90 (2)
Thomas A223 (3)
Hudson, Mrs. Esther A460
Hellen A372
Henry A90 (2) A460 (2)
Joseph A434
Mrs. Mary A145
Obadiah A223 A460 (2)
Richard A375
SARAH A92
Hulbert, Mrs. Jerusha A504 (2)
John A287 (3)
Mrs. Prudence AI27
Hulbut, Mrs. Jerusha A604 (2)
Hulse, Caleb M. A375 (3)
Caleb Mapes A94 (3)
Gilbert A426 (2)
Henry AI37 (2)
Isaac A94 AI57
Huntting, John A7 AI98
William A7
Hutchinson, Benjamin A429
Elizabeth AI64 (2)
Ely AI64
Hannah AI64
Mrs. Hannah AI64 (2)
Henry AI64
John AI64
Mehitabel AI64
Mrs. Phebe AI64 (2)
Mrs. Phebe AI64
SAMUEL A164 (5) A510
Ireland, Daniel A320
Mrs. Elizabeth A320
Jacob A320 (3)
John A320
JOSEPH A320
Joseph Jr. A320 (3)
Losee A320

Thomas Al5 (2) Al49 (2)
Al69 (2) A295 A320
Isaacs, Aaron A510
  Aaron Jr. A354
  Isaac A510
  Mary A510 (2)
  Mrs. Phebe A510
  Samuel A510
Jackson, Amy A455
  Mrs. Sarah A512
Jacobs, Joseph A476 (2)
Jagger, Abigail A89 A435
  Anna A47 (2) A435
  David A435 (2)
  Enoch A435 (4) A460 (2)
  Hanna A435
  Jonathan A435 (2)
  Mrs. Miriam A435
  Mrs Mehetable A460
  Miriam A435
  Mrs. Miriam A435
  Silvanus A330
  STEPHEN A227 (2) A435
  Susanna A435
  Mrs. Susannah A479
  Widow Al45
Jarvis, Austin A59
  Mrs. Charity A45 A413 (2)
  Isaiah A413
  JONATHAN A413
  Juliana A496
  Phebe A413
  Rebakar A428
  Robert A247
  Seth A233 (2)
  Timothy A413
  William A39 A413
Jayne, Bathsheba A41 0
  Ebenezer A41 0
  Elizabeth Al32

Mrs. Elizabeth A132
Isaac A290
JOHN Al60
JOSEPH A410
Mrs. Mary Al60 (4) A290
(2)
Micah Al60 (2)
Morris A290 A410
Peter A410
Robert Sr. Al07 (2)
SAMUEL Al32 (5)
Stephen A410
Mrs. Tabitha A410 (3)
William Jr. Al32 (2)
Jennings, Mrs. Abigail A504
  Jasper A29
  Mrs. Mary Al21
  Samuel A24 (2)
  Thomas A200
  Silvanus A200
Jervis, Eliphalat A22 (2)
  A206 (4)
  John A428
  Mrs. Phebe A247
  Mrs. Sarah A320
Jesseup, Ebenezer A25A235
  (2)
  Matthew A287 (2)
  Thomas A235
  Thomas Jr. A235 (2)
  Zebulon A200 (2)
Johnes, Gardiner A210
  OBADIAH A210
  Thomas A210
  William A210 (3)
Johnson, Mrs. Abigail A467
  Dorian A455 (2)
  Mrs. Hester A455
  Reuben Al72
Johnston, Heathcote

Jones, Mr. A97
  Eleazer A48
  Elias A263 A441
  Elizabeth A263 (3) A441
  (3) A510 Mrs. Hannah
  A263
  Joan AI03
  Jonathan AI87
  Mrs. MARY A263 (2) A441
  Paul A263
  Mrs.Tabitha A410
  Thomas A7 (2) A48
  WILLIAM A263 (2)
Keen, Rosana A43
Kelcy, John A229 (2)
Kellam, Jesse A80
  Joshua A80
Kelley, Shadrack AI17
Kennedy, James A293
Ketcham, Carll AI14 (2) A219
  (2)
  Conkling A59 (2) A203
  Jemima A241
  John AI72 (2) A203 (2)
  A243 (2) A273 (2) A293
  (2) A316 (2) A413
  Jonathan Smith A374
  Mary AI56
  Mrs. Phebe A374 (2)
  Philip A59 (2)
  Samuel A349
  Selah A241 (2)
  Solomon A59 A203 A316
  (2)
  Mrs.Susannah A341
Kettletas, Mrs. Charity AI05
  Garret AI05
King, Abigail A267
  Abraham A362 (2)
  ASA A462

Daniel A300
Ephraim A27 (2)
Gamaliel A444
Gilbert A267
JOHN A267 (4)
Joseph A267
Mrs. Mary A462
Mehitable A267 A272
Nathaniel A267 (2) A462
(2)
Nathaniel Jr. A379 (2)
Mrs. Phebe A267
Rufus A267 (3)
Samuel A462
Kinner, Jeremiah A432 (2)
  Jonathan A432
  Mrs. Mary A432
  Phebe A432
  Selah A432 (2)
  WILLIAM A432 (2)
Landon, Bethiah A41 (2)
  Elijah A41 (2)
  Jared A41 (2) A461 A925
  (2)
  Mary A41 (2)
Lane, Mrs.JEREMIAH A24
  Daniel A354
  David AI64
  John AI3 (2) AI03 (4) A289
  (2)
Lefferts, Leffert A300
Lefford, Adam AI67
  Hermon A320
Lester, Sylvester A462 A495
  (2)
Lewis, Asenth A80
  Daniel A80
  Eleanor A80
  Henry Scudder A229 (2)
  A408

James Jr. A455
John A80
Joseph A90 A219 (2)
A413
Mrs. Mary A455
Mrs. Nancy A80
SAMUEL A80
Thomas Bunce A80
L'Hommedieu, Benjamin
A312 (2)
EPHRAIM AI23 A384
Ezra A257 (2) A282 (2)
Mrs. Mehitable A384 (2)
Nancy, A384
Samuel A384 (4) A386 (2)
A484 A521
Mrs. Sarah A386 A434
L'Honneur, Mrs. RACHEL
AI05 A488
Long, James A205
Longbottom, Jacob A97
JOSHUA A325
Julianah A325
Lary A325 (3)
Serah A325
Loper, Abraham A162 (2)
Amos AI62
Amus AI62
Cloe AI47
DANIEL A147 A162 (2)
Henry AI62
Hinry AI62
JAMES A162 (2)
Jason AI A352
Jeremy AI62
Joel A147
Mrs. Mary AI47 (2) AI62
(2)
Mercy A471
Phebe AI62

William AI62
Luce, Abraham A280 (2)
David A280
ELEAZER A280 (2)
Elizabeth A280
Mahetabal A280
Mrs. Mehetabel A280 (3)
A310
Ludlam, Anthony A495
Ludle, Hennery A20
Ludlow, Henry A222
Ludlum, Anthony L495
Fanny A509
Henry A20 (2)
Jeremiah A509 (2)
Lupton, Christopher A200
DAVID A495 (4)
Rebecca A495*
Lyons, Anna A217 (2)
JAMES A217
John A217
Joseph A217 (2)
Thomas A217 (8)
Lysaght, William A22 (2)
A206 (2)
McAdam, Mrs. Gloriana
Margaretta AI05
John Loudon AI05 (3)
Mackie, George A66 AI19 (2)
Mrs. Hannah A123
Malcolm, Hugh A394
Mason. Lucretia A89
Matthews, Elias A253 (2)
A328 A352 A399 A434
A523
Merrit, John A76 (2)
Miller, Mr. A97
Abraham A48 (3) AI82 (2)
A300 A493
Ananias A48

Benejah S. A134
Betsy A488
Burnet A7 (2) A48 A354
Clarissa Al34
Daniel A211 (2)
David A300
Deliverance A488 (2)
EBENEZER Al02 (2) Al34
A334
ELEAZER A48 (2)
Elisabeth A488
Elizabeth A337
Huntting A21 (2) 354 (3)
Isaac Al34 (2) A334 (3)
A488
JEREMIAH A48 A354 (4)
Joanna A488 A493
Joel A493
JOHN A211 (5) A300
A334
John Jr. A7
Joseph A488 (3)
Keturah A488
Kiturah A488
Lewis A211 (2)
Mrs. Martha Al34
Mary A85
Nathaniel Al34 (2) Al62
A488 (2) A493 (3)
Phebe A85 A493
Rachel A493 (2)
Mrs. Rebakah A211 (2)
Richard A488
Mrs. Ruth A354 (3)
Mrs. Sarah Al34
Silvanus A354
Susanah A85
TIMOTHY A488 (6)
URIAH A399 A493 (2)
Mrs. Uriah A493 (3)

Zadock A211
Zophar A488 (3)
Zophar Al34
Mills, George A357 (2)
Israel A360 (2)
Jacob A360 (2)
Mrs. MARY A360
Micah Al87 A208
Samuel A360
Mrs. Tabitha A357 (2)
William A260 A360 (2)
Mitchell, Mrs. Temperance
A523
Mogar, Christopher A497
Moger, John A601
Monfoort, Garret A306 (3)
Moore, Benjamin A67
Calvin A267 (2) A382 (2)
DANIEL A253 (2) A523
David A253
James Al96 (2)
Joseph A253
Nathan A9
Silas A253
Simon A9
Stephen A253
Thomas A282
More Calvin A267 (2)
Morgan, Mrs. Elizabeth A22
(3)
JOHN A22
Morgin, Elizabeth A22 (3)
Moubray, Anning A420 A524
Mount, Thomas A73
Mowbray, Annin A420 A524
Mrs. Phibe A524
Muirson, George A5 A73
A325
Mrs. Mary A325 (3)
Mulford, Abigail Al30

ABRAHAM AI30 (4) A493
(2)
Mrs. Abraham AI30
David AI32 (3)
Elisabeth A510 (2)
Elisha A354
Huntting A354
John A298
Jonathan AI64 (2)
Josiah A293 A510
Lemuel AI30
Mary AI30
Mrs. Mary AI64
Phebe A127
Rebakah AI30
Samuel AI30 (3)
Timothy A7
William A37
Newnan, Silas AI14
Newton, BENJAMIN A434
Caleb A440
James A434
John A434 (3) A448 (3)
Mrs. Mary A434
Nicoll, Mr. AI80
Mrs. Frances A450 (2)
Joanna Rachal AI05
WILLLAM A450 (3)
Nic(h)oll, Benjamin A450
Elizabeth A233 (2)
Henry A450 (2)
Samuel A233
Nickerson, Abigail A521
ENSIGN A521
James A521 (2)
Tabitha A521
Mrs.Tabitha A521 (2)
Norris, Alice AI26
JOHN AI 26 (4) A329
Mrs. Sarah AI26

Norton, Timothy AI17
Nostran, Charity A318
Daniel A456
Foster A318
Jacobus A55 (2) A245 (2)
Mrs. Phebe A55
Nostrand, Charity A318
Nostron, Daniel A456
Oakes, Ephraim A149 (2)
Oakley, John AI12 (2) AI52
(2) A245 (2) A247 A320
(2) A456 A532 (2) Mrs.
Phebe A320
Mrs. Rebeckah A243
Richard, A416
Samuel A243 (2) A247
A416 (2)
William T. A247
Wilmot A55 (2) AI52 (2)
A318 (2)
Ogden, Betsy A273
Mrs. Hannah A273
Mary A273
Robert A273 (2)
Sarah A273
Mrs. Sarah A273
Osborn, Abraham A7 (2)
Conkling A7
Cornelius A7
Daniel A402 (3)
Daniel Jr. A67 (2)
Jacob A7
Jane A7
Jeremiah A7 (2)
Lewis A7
Mary A87 (2) A402
Phebe A7
Mrs. Phebe A7
THOMAS A7 (3)
Overton, Agatha A315

Agurty A315
Benjamin A82 A375
David A94
Deborah A82
Elten A69
JAMES A82
John A9 (2) A94 (2)
Justus A82 (2)
Messenger A32 (2)
Nathaniel A82 (2) A94 (2)
Palmer A94 (2)
Mrs. Phebe A82 (2)
Owen, ABIJAH A497
Cata A497
Elisabeth A497
Mrs. Elizabeth A497 (2)
James A497
John A497
Micah A497 (2)
Paine, Benjamin A67
Palmer, Mrs. Sarah A518
Parker, Deborah A27
Mrs. Hannah A27
James A476
Maria A476 (2)
Mrs. Phebe A476 (2)
Parmelee, Mrs. Phebe AI76
Parshall, Elias A312
Parsons, Abigail A300
Mrs. Abigail A300 (2)
Andrew A300
Chatfield A300
Mrs. Deborah A298
Eli AI98 (3) A276 (2)
Elnathan A276 A300 (3)
Grandfather AI64 (2)
Hannah AI98
Hedges,A300
Henry A298
Jehiel A300

Jeminah AI98
Jeremiah A298 (4)
Mrs. Joanna A300
JOHN AI98 A298 A300 (2)
Ludlam A87 (2) A298 (2)
Mary AI98
Mrs. Mary AI98 (3)
Merrey AI98 (3)
Puah AI98
Robert AI64 AI98 (2) A298
(4)
Robert Jr. A300 (2)
SAMUEL AI 98 (4)
Mrs. Sarah A523
Seth A300 (5)
Stephen A276 (2) A300
Pearsall, Daniel A45
David A456
Elias A312
Peases, Matthew A223 (2)
Peck, Mrs.Experience A219
(3)
Pedrie, John A293
Peirson, Daniel A474
Jedidiah A474
Penney, Benjamin AI89 A464
(3)
EDWARD A464
Petersen, LAWRENCE A466
(2)
Lorrence A464 (2)
Olowf A466
Petty, Mrs. Anna A253
Mrs.Easter A310
Ezekiel A925
James A525
Jeremiah A525
Phenix, Alexander A273
Daniel A273
Elizabeth A273

Mrs.Elizabeth A273
Jonnet A273
Rebecca A273
Sidney A273
Phillips, Amy A501
Charity A501
Deborah A390 (2)
Fredrick A501
George A390
Hannah A247
Jonas A390
Josiah A534
MICAH A390
SAMUEL A501 (4)
Temperance A501
William A208 (2), A466 (2)
Pierson (see Peirson)
Catherine A50
Daniel A50
David A50 (3) A518 (2)
Elias AI45
Elizabeth A253
Mrs. Elizabeth A253 (2)
Mrs. Eunice A240
Mrs. Hannah A518
JOB A50
John A50
Lemuel A50 (3)
Margaret A71 A394 (2)
Martha A394 (2)
Peleg A518
Prudence A253
Rebekah A394
Samuel A50
Sarah A394 (2)
SILVANUS A394
Timothy A394 (3) A518
Platt, Amos A316
Ebenezer A219 (2) A229
(2) A273(3) A406 (2)

Mrs. Esther A229
Mrs. Hannah A243
JACOB AI49 (2)
Jeremiah A273 (2)
Jesse AI74
John AI12 AI72
Joseph AI49 (2) A241 (2)
A295 (2) Philip AI72 (2)
Rebekah A295
Mrs. Rebecca A241
Mrs. Sarah A247
Scudder A229
Selah AI72
Zebulon A413 (3)
Zophar A273 A413 (3)
Zophar Jr. A219 (2) A243
A293 (2)
Post, Mrs. Abigail A452
Bethiah A504 (2)
Charity A240
Deborah A240
HENRY A240 (2)
Mrs.Henry A240 (2)
Isaac A32 (2) AI19 A238
James A238
Jeremiah A236 (2) A240
(2) A279 (2) John Jr. A145
(2)
Mrs. Mehitable A479
Samuel A479
Mrs. Sarah A479
Stephen A240 (4)
Potter, Elisabeth A34
Powell, Amos A76
JOSEPH A76 (2)
Samuel A76 (2)
Punderson, George Muirson
AI07 (2) AI17
Raiment, Mrs. Elizabeth AI72
Ranger, Mrs. Elizabeth A300

Samuel A300
Rapalye, John Jr. A450
Rayner, Donijah A263
    Joel A332
    Josiah A534
    Stephen A330
Raynor, Esther A435
    Hugh A435 (2)
    James A435 (2)
Reeve, Mrs. Anna AI37 (3)
    Barnabas AI78
    Charles A452
    Daniel AI78 (2)
    David AI43
    Experience AI78(2)
    Hannah AI78
    Harmoy AI37
    Isaac AI37 A428
    Isaac Tuthill A312 (2)
    A315 (4)
    ISAIAH A208 (2) A452
    JAMES A2 AI37 (4) AI78
    A220
    Mrs. Joanna A312
    Joel A452
    John AI37 (4) A143 (3)
    A173 (3) A328
    Joshua A323 (2)
    Juliana A452
    Kezia(h) AI78 A223
    Mrs. Kezia AI78 (3)
    Mrs. Mary A123
    Nathaniel A287
    Paul Jr. A214
    Sarah AI78 (2) Silas A452
    (3)
    STEPHEN A143
    THOMAS AI78 (4)
    Timothy A280
Remp Michael A243

Reynolds John A503 (2)
Rhinelander, William AI05 (3)
Ricklow, Jacob A528
Riker, John A450
Robbins, Isaac AI03 (2) AI07
    (4)
    Joseph A303
    Scudder A76 (2)
    Mrs. Suzannah A107 (2)
    Van Hackly A229
    Van Haelah A229 A428
    (2)
    ZEBULON AI07 (3)
Robert, Daniel A208 (2)
Robinson, Mrs. Elizabeth
    A469
    JOHN A469 (3)
    Jonathan A296
    Richard A469 (3)
    THOMAS A486
Roe, Anne AI9
    Asel AI9
    Austin A325 (2)
    Mrs. Charity A97 (2)
    Deborah A97 (2)
    Elisabeth A97 (2)
    Hannah A97 (3)
    James A97 AI02 A406
    JOHN AI9 (2) A97 (2)
    A325
    Justus AI9 (2)
    Martha A360
    Mary AI9
    Nancy A4
    NATHANIEL A97 (3)
    NATHANIEL JR AI02
    Mrs. Nathaniel Jr. AI02 (2)
    Philip AI9 (3) A97 (5) A360
    (2) A493 (2)
    Philip Jr. A97

Mrs. Ruth AI9 A325
Sarah A97(3)
Thomas A406(2)
William A97
Rogers, Abigail A507
Abraham A308 (2)
Caleb A308 (2)
Deborah A245
Ebenezer A245
Elizabeth A245 A295
Mrs. Elisabeth A399 A507 (3)
Epenetus A295
Experience AI49 A229
Hannah A507
Herrick A507 (2)
JACAMIAH AI5 (3)
Mrs. Jacamiah A15
Jacob AI49
Jemima AI12
Jerusha A534
Jervis A245
JESSE AI12 (2),A534 (3)
Job A534
Joel A229 A344
JOHN AI12 (2) A222 A245 (4) A295
Jonah AI (2) A22
Jonathan A63 (2) AI12 A295 A430 (2) A481 A492 (2) A503 (2)
JOSEPH A295 A534 (2)
Joshua A85 A295 (2)
JOSIAH AI5 A229
Mrs. Josiah A229 (2)
Keturah AI5
Levinah A295
Mrs. Marcy AI12 (2)
Mrs. Matha Stuart A308
Mary AI49 A245 A507

Mrs. Mary A210 A308 (2)
Medad A229 (2)
Melancthon A229 (4)
Mrs. Mercy AI12 (2)
NATHANIEL A308 A430
Nehemiah AI67
NOAH A295
Obadiah A330
Phebe A245 A347
Platt A229 (3)
Rachel A229 A534
Rebecca AI5
Robert AI5 A229 A344 (3)
Ruth AI5 A295 (2)
Mrs. Ruth A245 (2)
Sarah AI56 (2) A492 (2)
Mrs. Sarah AI69 (2) A241 A534 (2)
Sceva A308 (2)
Seth A295
Stephan AI23
Susanna A507
Thomas AI5 (2) A229 (2)
William A229 A430
Zachariah A245 (2)
Zebulon Whitman A245
ZEPANIAH A507
Rolph, Benjamin A243
David A243
Mrs. Mary A55
MOSES A243
Phebe A243
Reuben A243 (3)
Rose, ABRAHAM A222 (4)
Mrs. Abraham A222 (4)
Clarissa A222
David AI21 (2) AI54 AI87 (2) A208 (2) A497 (2)
Esther AI87
Rufus A222

103

Samuel H. A394 (3) A476
A521
Samuel Hains A222 (3)
Rowe, Martha A360
Thomas A406 (2)
Rudyard, Thomas A392
William A260 A392
Ruland, David A55
Mrs. Jerusha Al56 (3)
John A55
Joseph A94
Rusco, David A413
David Jr. A219 (2) A243
Mrs. Jemima A59
Rusel, Mr. A518
John A50
Sage, Ebenezer Al64 (2)
Salmon, Joshua A372 (2)
Joshua Jr. Al91
Sammis, Augustain A205
Deborah A205
Hannah A205
Jarvis A205 (2)
Job A243
John Al72 A205
Mrs. Martha A416
Mary Al72 A205
Olly A205
Mrs. PHEBE Al72
Phebe A205
Ruth A205
Sarah A205:
Mrs. Sarah A205
Susannah A205 (2)
WILLIAM A205 (3)
Sandford, Abegall A396
Benjamin Al76
Bethuel Al 76
Daniel A85 (2) A503 (2)
DAVID Al76 A352 (2)

Elias Al76 A523 (2)
Elihu A509
Mrs. Elizabeth A408 (3)
Elisha A443
EZEKIEL Al76 (4) A352
Hamutal A509
Hezekiah Al76
JAMES A43 (2) A408
A509
James Montgomery, A53
Jane A352
Jared A509
JOEL A409
Mrs. Joel A509
John Monmoth A53
Josiah A176
Lemuel A509 (3)
Lewis A352 (4)
Mrs. MARTHA A53
Mrs. Mary A308
Matthew A352
Nathan A85 (2) A430
Oliver A509
Phebe A85 (2) A430
Mrs. PHEBE A85 (3) A430
Prudence A509
Sarah A53 (2)
Mrs. Sarah Al76
THOMAS A85 (3) A222
Zachariah A452 (2) A484
Zecharias A484
Saterly, Daniel A90 (2)
Satherly, Margaret A50
Satterly, Daniel A73 (3)
Saxton, Daniel Al80 (2)
John Al80 (2)
Sayre, Mr. A479
Abigail A328
Mrs. Abigail A495
Abraham Al19 (3) Al43 (2)

A200 (2)
BENJAMIN A328
Mrs. Bethiah Al19
David A64 (2) A253 (2)
A328 (5)
Elizabeth Al19 A328
Hannah Al19
Mrs Huldah A507
James Al19 A328 (5)
A476 (2)
Jane Al19 A235
John Al19 (2) A263
Joshua Al46 (3)
Mrs. Mary A235
Merit A507
NEHEMIAH Al19
Phebe A328
Polly A476
Mrs. Prudence A476
Susannah A328
Thomas A507
Zephaniah A328
Schellinger, David A523
Scidmore, Mrs. HANNAH
A233
Isaac A233 (3)
Joel A36
Joseph A233
Mrs. Margaret A36 (3)
PHILIP A36
Platt A36
Scott, Deborah A200
JACKSON A200
Mrs. Jackson A200
Mary A200
Mathew A200
Samuel A200
Sarah A200
Temperance A200
Thomas A200

Scribmore, Mrs. Deborah
A241
Scribner, Jesse Bunce A530
Luri A530
Seth Al10 (2)
Scudder, Hannah A59
Henry A36 (2) A59 (3)
Al14 (2) Al92 Al95 (2)
A344 (2) A424 A467 A530
Henry Jr. A467 A530 (2)
Jacob A210
Jesse A59 (2)
Joel A59
John A57 (2) A59 (3)
Mrs. REBECCAR A428
(2)
Sarah A59
Mrs. Sarah A59
TIMOTHY A59 (2) Al 92
Tredwell A59 (2) A247
Young P. A467 (2)
Seaman, Jacob A388 A512
Sell, Mrs. Jemima Al69 (2)
Wessell A469 (2)
William A375
Seward, Mrs. Anne A479
Shaw, DANIEL A272 (2),
A444 (4) A445 (4)
Hannah A444 A445
Josiah A444 (2) A445
Mrs. MARY A444
Shelton, William Al17
Sherril, Abraham A493
Daniel Al (2)
Short, Mary A315
Skillman, Mrs. Jerusha A229
Joseph Al92 (2)
Thomas A229
Smith, ABRAHAM AllO
Addam A349 (2)

Alexander A349 (2)
Ame A532 (2)
Amos A217 (3) A290 (2)
Amos Jr. A290 (2)
Anne A456
Mrs. Anna A269 (2) A339
Barnabas Al10 (2)
BENJAMIN A180 (2) A374
Caleb A515 (2)
Caleb Jr. A369
Catharine A374 (2)
Mrs. Catharine A374
Charity A515
Charles A269
Charlotte A20
DANIEL A392
David A349 (4)
Dorcus Al56
Elias A349
Elizabeth Al43
Mrs. Elizabeth Al10 A320
Epenetus A36 (2) A39 (2)
A213 A339 (2) A334
Eunice A374 (2)
Every A94
Ezekiel A260
Fanny A94
Frederick A467
Freelove Al80
Hannah Al60 (2)
Mrs. Hannah A293 (2)
A467
Henrv A334
Henry Jr. A229
Hezekiah A467
Hubal A243
HUGH A269
ISAAC A39 A94 (4) A203
(3) A410 (2)
Mrs. Isaac A94

Isaiah A349
Israel Al80 (3)
Jacob A203 (2) A467 (3)
James Al80 (3) A374 (2)
A375
James III A375 (2)
Jane AllO
Japhat A94
Jeremiah A530
JESSE A203 (3) A375
Joanna Al57
JOB A213
John A94 A213 (2) A389
(2) A357(2) A532
JONAH Al57
Jonas A515 (3)
JONATHAN A374 A376
Joshua A94 (5) A515 (2)
Mrs. Joshua A94
Josiah A80 (2) A269 (2)
Lucius A349 (4)
Margaret A94
Martha A369 (2)
Mrs. Martha A94
Mary A213 A349
Mrs. Mary A456
MICAH A392 (3) A515
Moses A213
NATHANIEL A20 A269 (2)
A515
Mrs. Nathaniel A20
Nicolas A213 (3)
Nicoll A269 (3)
OBADIAH A339 A349
A392 (2)
Paul Theodore A369
Peter A375
Philetus A217 (3) A392 (2)
Philip Al7 A20 (2) A80 (2)
Prior A349

106

Puah A90
Rachel A20 A375
Mrs. Rachel A375 (2)
Richard A456 A515
Ruth Al60 A374
Mrs. Ruth A229 A241
Samuel Al80 A349
Sarah A20 A375
Mrs. Sarah A203 A349
Siah A349
Mrs. Survillah Al57 (3)
Mrs. Susanah A349 A467
(3)
Mrs. Tabitha A392 (3)
Temperance A374
Thomas A251 (2) A349
Timothy A374 (2)
Walter A20
William Al10 (2) A159
A18O A269 A349(2) A466
Woodhull A392
Zachariah A243
Zedock A80 (2)
Zebulon A203 (3)
Zephaniah A374 (3)
Snedecor, John A152
Soper, Allexander A486 (2)
Amos A436 (2)
Elizabeth A486
Mrs. Elizabeth A486
John A486 (2) A524 (2)
Mary A486
Phebe A486
Squier, Jonathan A386 (2)
Squires, John Al67
Jonathan A386 (2)
Thomas Al67
Stephens. Mrs. Abigail A332
Steward, Silia A255
Stewart, Silas A484 (2)

Stratton, Benjamin A3O0
Daniel A430
David A354
John A48 (2) A57 (2) A87
(2) Al30 Al92 (2) Al95 (2)
Al98 (2) A298 A367 A493
Mrs. Mary A312 (2)
Strong, Justice A97
BENEJAH A420 (2)
Mrs. Elisabeth A420
Hannah A420
Mary A420
Nancy A420
Samuel Thompson A420
(4)
Selah A73 (2) Al17 (2)
Al54 A290 A439 (2)
Silas C. A420
Thomas Al17 (2)
William A420
Stuward, Silia A255
Sumrick, Mary Al3
Swasey, Mrs. Hannah A377
Swazey, Daniel A289 (2)
Sweasy, Richard A312
Swezey, ABEL A5 (2) Al59
Daniel A289 (2)
Mrs. Elizabeth A5
Ezekiel A5 (2)
Mrs. Hannah A377
Jeremiah A5 Al59
Mrs. Jerutia A5 (2)
Mulford A5 (2)
Richard A312
Stephen Al59 Al86 (2)
William A5 (2) Al86 (2)
Sylvester, Brindley A257
Symmes, Anne (Anny) A315
(2)
Tallmadge, Benjamin A97 (3)

David Jr. A147 (2)
Dayton A303
Mrs. Jemima A48
John A97
Mary A441
Susanna A97
Thomas A48
Zipporah A97
Taylor, Hannah A367
Jonas A367
Mordecai A367
Mrs. Tabitha A367
WILLIAM A367
Terrell, BARNABUS Al37
A223
Terry, Abigail Al91 A276
Anna A276
Bethiah A495
DANIEL Al91 (2) A214
A272
Daniel Jr. A272 (2)
Hannah A423
Henry A214 (2)
James Al91 (3) A276
JEREMIAH A276 (2) A300
Mrs. Jeremiah A276 (2)
John A276 (3) A423 (2)
John C. Al96 (2)
Jonathan Al03
Joseph A379
Louisa Al91
Martha A276
Mary Al91
Mrs. Mary Al91 A365
Mehitable A276
Patience A423
Mrs. Patience A312 A423
(2)
ROBERT A423
Samuel A276

William Al91 A372 A450
Thompson, Isaac A420 A450
Jonathan A498
Mary A408 (2)
Samuel A439 A408 (2)
Tillinghart, John A300
Puah A300
Thomas A300
Titus, Jacob A43
John A43
Jonathan A43 (2)
Tooker, Mr. A97
Caturah A251
NATHANIEL Al9 Al17 (2)
A426(2)
Mrs. Ruth Al17
Thomas Al17
William A434 (2)
Topping, Daniel A474 (2)
DAVID A50 A474
Mrs. Jane A474
Matthew A474 (3)
Mrs. Prudence A365
Stephen S. A53
William A328
Totten, Edmond A367 (2)
Polly A307
Simeon A367 (2)
Townsend, Hennery A341 (2)
Tredwell, Thomas Al69
Turell, BARNABUS A223
Turner, Mrs. Sr. A13
Mrs. Catherine Al3 (2)
Henry Al3
John Al3 (2)
WILLIAM Al3 (4) A466 (2)
Tuthill, Abraham A267 (2)
A462 (2)
Barnabas A462
Daniel A379 A462 (2)

David A267 A377 (3)
Mrs. Elisabeth A377
Harmony A377
HENRY A315
Isaiah A272 (2)
JAMES Al91 A312 (2)
A377 (4)
Mrs. Jemima A534
JOHN A377 (2) A379 (5)
Mrs. John A379
Jonathan Al98, A300 (2)
Joshua A372 (2)
Mrs. Mary A312
Nathaniel A267 (2)
Mrs. Phebe A315 (2)
Mrs.Temperance A312
Tyler, Mrs. Hannah A410
Udall, Charles A78 (2) A512
Daniel A512 (2)
JOSEPH A512
Nathaniel A295 (2)
Mrs. Phebe A512
Richard A78 A512 (5)
Richard Sr. A78 (2)
Sarah A78 A512
Mrs. Sukey A78 (2)
THOMAS A20 A78 A512
William A512 (2)
Udle, Nathaniel A295 (2)
Underhill, Andrew Al05 (2)
Mrs. Mary A73
Vail, Mrs. Deborah A57
Mrs. Elizabeth A282 (2)
Mrs. Hannah A69
John A57 (3) A344 A367 (2)
Mrs. Keziah A206
Mrs. Mary A69 Micah A57 (4)
MOSES A52

Platt Jr. A86 (2)
Silas A382
Thomas Jr. A379
Valentine, Charles A78 David A78
Mrs. Esther A318
Gilbert A318
Jacob Jr. A78 (2)
JOB A455
Lewis A78
NATHAN A318
Richard A3[0 (4) A455 (6)
Scudder A318
Vance, Mrs. Keturah A495
Vandewater, John A455
Mrs. Mary A455 (2)
Van Scoy, Isaac A300
Van Wikes, Theodorus A247
Warner, Benjamin A2
DANIEL A2
David A2 Al96 (2)
Deborah A2
Mrs. Hannah A2 (2)
James A2
Mehetabel A2
Webb, Mrs. Elisabeth A382
Jonathan A497
Orange A382
Thomas A461
Wells, Mrs. Abigall A214
Mrs. Bethiah A69
Calvin A461
DANIEL A2 (2) A214 (2)
A216 (2) A272 (3) A310
A312 (5)
DAVID A214 (2) A261 (2)
A312 (2)
Elijah A272 A312
Elisha A272
Elizabeth A296

Giles A496 (2)
Hannah A225 (2) A29 (2)
A525(2)
HENRY A298
ISAIAH A272 (2) A312 (2)
Mrs. Isaiah A272 (2)
James A214 A525
Jeremiah A225 (2) 312
A525
Mrs. Joanna A214 A312
JOHN Al 89 (3) A261
A525 (2)
Joseph A296
Manly Al89 (2) A214 (4)
Martha Al89
Mary Al89 A272 A315
A525
Mrs. Mary Al89 A525 (2)
Mehetabel A214
Naomi A296 (2)
Nathanial A225 (2) A261
Nathaniel Jr. A312 A444
Obadiah A296 (3) A447
(2)
Mrs. Sarah A961 (3)
Thomas Dickinson A296
(2)
TIMOTHY Al89 A525 (2)
Wetmore (Whitmore)
Appolos A439
Irene A439
June A439
NOAH A439 (3)
Samuel Ithiel A439
Mrs. Submit A439 (2)
Wheeler, Mrs. Phebe Al72
Wheler, Platt Al12 (2)
Sarah Al12
White, CHARLES A386
BENEZER A29 A394

Father A516
Henry A24 (2) A330 (2)
A332 (2) A339
Israel A416 (4)
James A29 (5) A516
James Jr. A516 (2)
JOSEPH A45 A247
Mrs. Mehetable A29 (2)
Mrs. Sarah A45 (2) A386
(2)
Silas A29 A516 (2)
STEPHEN A416
Steven A45
Whitfield, George A435
Whitman, Isac A247
Jarvis A45
Jesse A247 (4)
John A247
Joseph A247
Nathaniel A320 (2) A416
Nathaniel Jr. A247 (2)
NEHEMIAH A247
Whitman, Mrs. Phebe A45
A247
Stephen A247 (3)
Whitson, Amos A45 (2)
John A45 (2)
Wickham, Anna A9
Mrs. Bethiah A223 (2)
John A223 (2)
Joseph Yarker A281 A460
A528
Mrs. Mary A372
Norris A461 (4)
Mrs. Norris A461
Phebe A528
Sally Al37 (2)
THOMAS A48 (2) Al82 (2)
A461 (3)
Wickes, AMBROSE A208 (2)

A369 (3)
Ambrous A208 (2)
Azariah A206 (2)
Charity A206
David A206
Jacob A312
Jemima A39
Mrs.JEMIMA A89
John A89 A312 A413 (2)
Jonas A206
Joseph A210 (2)
Joshua A369 (3)
JOSIAH A369
Lemuel A369 (2)
Mary A206
Mrs. Mary A172
Moses A369 (3)
Obadiah A210 (2)
Phebe A498
Mrs. Phebe A206 (2)
Persiller A206
Priscilla A206
Rachel A515
Mrs. Sarah A369 (2)
Seth A369 (2)
Solomon A369
Thomas A243
Wiggins, Daniel A22 A293
Matthew Bunce A293
Richard A247
Willets, Amos A524
Amos Jr. A486 (2)
Mrs. Deborah A512
Isaac AI59 (2) A524 (3)
Jacob A20 (2)
JOHN A20 A524
Jonah A512
Samuel A524 (3)
Williams, Austin A465
William A455

Williamson, David A444 (2)
Elisabeth A24
Jedidiah A20 A426 (2)
Mrs. Jemima A24
John A315 (2)
William Lane A24
Wilson, John A293
Wood, David A36
Epenetus A39 (2)
ISRAEL A219 A243 A413
Mrs.Israel A219 (2)
Mrs. Ruth AI52 (2)
Samuel AI74 A219 (2)
A320 (2)
Selah A45 (2) A416 (2)
A456
Woodhull, Abraham A73 (3)
A217 A251 (2)A290 (2)
A339 (2) A439 (2)
Abraham Cooper A325
CALEB AI34 (2) A334 (3)
A337
David A337 (2)
Dorothy A73
Elizabeth A334
Mrs. Elizabeth A289
Gilbert A334 (2)
James A334 (2) A469
Jeffery Amherst A334 (2)
A337 (2)
JOHN A334 (2)
John Jr. A469
Julia A73
Mrs. Margaret A73 (2)
Mrs. Mary A339
Merit (Merrett) Smith A134
(2) A334 (4) A337 (2)
Nathaniel A251 (2) A423
Nathaniel Jr. A325
RICHARD A73 (2) AI87

A208
Robert A423
Sarah A73 A488
Susanna A73
William A334 A337
Woodruff, Mrs. Abigail A208
Abraham A255
Benjamin A255 A476
DAVID A365
Elias A365 (2)
Elizabeth A208 A255
Mrs. Elizabeth A365
Hallsey A365
Harriet A365
Isaac A208
James Al87 A365
Jehiel A208
Jesse A265 (2) A365 (2)
JOHN A235 (2)
Joshua A355
Mary A208 A255
MATTHEW A187 (3)
A208
NATHANIEL A197 A208
(2)
Phebe A208
Rebeacah A255
Sarah A255
Silas A365 (2)
Silas Jr. A365 (2)
Sylvester A365
Temperance A365
Woolworth, Aaron A64
Wright, John A392
Obadiah A507
Thomas A167
York, James Al5
Youngs, Abraham A214
Mrs. Anna A312
Benjamin A282

Mrs. Catharine A458 (3)
Christopher A280
Daniel A445 (2)
DAVID A458 (2)
Hannah Rachel A282
JAMES A2 (2) A214 (6)
Jeremiah A310
John A282 (3)
Joshua A257 A282 (4)
Josiah A444
Mrs. Lydia A379
Mary A282 (3) A444
Mrs. Mehetabel A214
Mrs. Rhoda A282
THOMAS A214 A282 (5)

Unidentified:
    -----, Rebecca A341

Indian:
    Jude A462

Negroes (male):
    Absalom A406
    Archibald A269
    Ben A269
    Bill Al92
    Cain A223
    Charles A293 A344 A515
    Comus A460
    Cuff A402
    Cyras A305
    Cyrus A365
    David A269
    Elijah A293
    Francis A339
    George A269 (2)
    Harry A349
    Isaac A315
    Jim Al92

Joseph A339
Lymas A90 (2)
Mingo A339
Peter A303
Petter A50
Reuben A392
Sam A269
Titus A269
Negroes (female):
Bette A349
Dawn A498
Dinah A303
Doll A269 A382

Fillis A290
Hagar A269
Jane A339
Jude A339
Moll Al05
Phillis A219
Rachel A365
Rhoda A293
Rose Al92
Sarah A339
Sib A269
Zipporah A339

www.ingramcontent.com/pod-product-compliance
Lightning Source LLC
Chambersburg PA
CBHW071140090426
42736CB00012B/2175